Final Fantasy V
Chris Kohler

Boss Fight Books
Los Angeles, CA
bossfightbooks.com

ISBN 13: 978-1940535-18-0
First Printing: 2017

Series Editor: Gabe Durham
Book Design by Cory Schmitz
Page Design by Christopher Moyer

In Japan, the word is always haunted by negative connotations. That belief is not common in America... In their yearning for Japan, they earnestly boast of being "otaku."

– Toshio Okada, 1995

their promise of being worth millions of dollars one unspecified day in the future.

Decades from now, one wall of every suburban Barnes & Noble will be devoted to a stunning array of Japanese *manga* in English translation, spanning genres from action to horror to romance to biography. Today, this is an impossible dream, and the portal to Japan that lives in this comic store is about one foot wide, and there are barely enough products to fill even this tiny shelf. These comics, with their inscrutable titles like *Urusei Yatsura*, are printed in black and white and cost twice as much money as their full-color American counterparts. VHS tapes of *anime*, too, are absurdly priced at $50 for barely an hour of animated content. You do not have $50, and YouTube is ten years away.

And yet, beckoning from the covers of these pricey treasures, come the intoxicating promises of stories and images and sensibilities that are nowhere to be found in any of the inexpensive domestic drafts that make up the other 99 percent of the comic store. A round-faced girl with green hair and tiny demon horns, barely fitting into a minuscule tiger-print bikini, beams flirtatiously at you. This is Japan, as far as you know. It is transfixing. America, its superheroes, and its pretzels and its Comics Code Authority, might well have crumbled away around you, for all you know in this moment.

JAPAN IS ANOTHER WORLD, separate from your own. It is not a place to which you can travel, but there are portals through which you can see it. These portals are imperfect; the image they return is distorted and superficial. It is your life's work to search for these portals, but there is only so much you can do at fourteen, without much ability to look for them outside your small town. But they still exist, even here.

One is in the Connecticut Post shopping mall in the city you were born: Enter through the ground floor, swing a left past the hot pretzels filling the aisle with their unmistakable cloying aroma that is the universal scent of "mall," past the arcade (itself the fuzziest of portals) and inside the comic book store, strategically placed at this well-trafficked intersection of video competition and warm mustard. It is 1995, and so the walls of this store are still papered with a plethora of foil-embossed, poly-bagged special editions of superhero comics, with

•

I don't know when I became aware that all of the video games I loved as a kid were coming from Japan, but it was well before I'd read my first manga, watched my first anime. I can certainly tell you of the first time I realized that something was being kept from me.

For the Nintendo Entertainment System-owning American kid of the 1980s, *Nintendo Power* was the Bible. Nintendo's in-house monthly magazine was not just holy text but also holy doctrine: We worshippers were offered an understanding of the world of Nintendo on a strictly need-to-know basis, and other sources were to be regarded with skepticism. Nintendo would pass to you the approved commandments, at the appointed hour, and never anything else.

One day in what must have been 1989, a third-grade classmate showed up with a video game magazine that was not *Nintendo Power*. I was only vaguely aware that these even existed, and I don't remember which magazine it was, although I think it may have been the first issue of *GamePro*. What I do remember is that he said it had pictures of *Super Mario Bros. 3*.

Bullshit, I thought, just as I had when another classmate said his uncle worked at Sega and had the unreleased "4D Glasses" for the Master System. No way did this kid's magazine have pictures of *Super Mario Bros. 3* when

Super Mario Bros. 2 had only just come out! But I looked at the two-page spread and my jaw dropped. There was Mario's next adventure, and the article said that it was already available for some game system in Japan called the "Famicom." It was in a magazine, so it must be true: *Super Mario Bros. 3* existed. Lucky-ass Japanese kids were playing it right now. And had I stayed in my *Nintendo Power* bubble, I'd have been none the wiser. These other magazines had some pretty ugly layouts and sloppy writing compared to *Nintendo Power*, and I'd come to learn that they often dealt in some sketchy rumors. But with that rawness came the unvarnished honesty of a staff that was not employed by the same company it reported on. They weren't keeping anything from me.

Poring over more issues of magazines like *Electronic Gaming Monthly* as the years went on, I slowly became aware that not only did Japan get the cool games *first*, sometimes Japan got games that we never got at all. Eventually those feelings of childhood jealousy turned into teenaged resentment: Why *didn't* we get these games? Why were we this second-rate video game dumping ground? Why did America suck so hard? Why couldn't I have been born in Japan?

And in 1995, the biggest perceived injustice, the game we should have gotten, the game I couldn't believe wasn't coming to America, was *Final Fantasy V.*

•

It should come as no surprise that a kid who was reading whatever manga he could possibly get his hands on was also deep into Japanese role-playing games. JRPGs, at that moment, represented the pinnacle of gaming for me. Japanese game developers had taken the tabletop swords-and-sorcery, hit-points-and-mana gameplay of Dungeons & Dragons and brought it into video games with their own unique flair. Final Fantasy in particular leaned hard into the storytelling aspect, crafting epic stories with symphonic soundtracks that took players on journeys that lasted dozens if not hundreds of hours. For a teen with no money and lots of free time, this was perfect.

Final Fantasy IV and *Final Fantasy VI* (originally released in America as *Final Fantasy II* and *Final Fantasy III* respectively) weren't just two of my favorite Super Nintendo games. They showed me things I didn't think video games could even do: Ambitious storytelling with compelling characters. Rich scores that made it sound like a tiny orchestra was trapped inside my SNES. Love. Humor. Death.

And there was a third game in that Super Famicom trilogy, the middle one, that was *supposed* to come out here. But it never showed up.

I didn't know the first thing about *Final Fantasy V*. But I knew we got hosed. Screwed over. And I wasn't going to let it slip away. This is how *Final Fantasy V* became the first game I ever imported from Japan. I didn't know the language, but that wasn't going to stop me. Soon, I'd find that others had the exact same idea.

Eventually, *Final Fantasy V* did get released in America: Seven years after its initial release, it was ported to Sony's PlayStation. But it was a game out of time, stuck with a pixelated, 2D, 16-bit aesthetic before pixels became cool again. A sloppy, rushed translation was the final nail in the coffin. In Japan, *Final Fantasy V* was a colossal hit, and is fondly remembered there today as one of the greatest games of the Super Famicom era. In America, it's considered the "black sheep" of the series, its rep totally ruined by a late, botched release.

In other words: We got a raw deal... but *Final Fantasy V* got a worse one. It's no black sheep. It might even be the best game in the whole series.

WORLD 1

"I HATED SCHOOL," the creator of Final Fantasy tells me. This interview was about to get interesting. I'd been writing about games for nearly two decades, and in that span of time had talked to many of my heroes, including Hironobu Sakaguchi. But by the time I'd first gotten to interview him, he'd already left the Final Fantasy series behind, and was on to new projects. So one thing I'd never gotten to do was to sit down with him and talk at length about old-school Final Fantasy. That all changed on a cool July afternoon in 2016, in the lobby of San Francisco's Argonaut Hotel.

Born in 1962, Sakaguchi says he of course watched a lot of anime on television growing up in Ibaraki prefecture north of Tokyo. But to understand what truly inspired his creative passions, he tells me, I have to know that he hated going to school.

"I would play hooky, and go out to the pachinko parlors," he said. And there he met a *pachi-puro*—a professional pachinko player—who started showing Sakaguchi the tricks of the trade. Pachinko machines, which look like small vertical pinball tables, are played by shooting piles and piles of tiny metal balls up into the playfield at a machine-gun clip, which then drop down a board filled with tiny pins—sort of like the game "Plinko" on *The Price is Right*. If the balls land in the right holes, you win... more balls, which you can exchange at a counter for prizes.

It would be illegal for the pachinko parlor to exchange those balls for cash. This is where Japan invokes the "Air Bud" rule: There's nothing in the rulebook that says a dog *can't* play basketball, and there's nothing in the law that says a pachinko parlor *can't* give you some otherwise worthless token as a prize that you can take across the street to a "separate" establishment that will exchange it for cash.

Sakaguchi may have hated class, but he was a quick study. The *pachi-puro* taught him how to shoot, how to aim, and what machines were most likely to pay out. In short order, teenage Sakaguchi was pulling down a pretty nice salary. "A hundred dollars a day," he says to me, switching briefly from Japanese to English, which he does when he really wants to make a point. A rare smile forms at the corner of his perpetually-mustachioed mouth. "I was rich."

Flush with cash, he ate up all the science fiction he could find. He'd watch movies like *Star Wars*, but he was also scooping up books by the shelf-ful. One smaller publisher, Hayakawa Bunko, was known for its deep fantasy and sci-fi catalogs, and he'd stand at the tiny Hayakawa shelf at the bookstores, devouring everything, imported and domestic alike. He was a fan of translated editions of *The Elric Saga* by Michael Moorcock, and also *Guin Saga*, a series of fantasy novels by the writer Kaoru Kurimoto. This was like Japan's own *Lord of the Rings*, a thrilling and violent fantasy series that eventually stretched to fill 150 volumes. Some of these volumes had covers illustrated by an artist named Yoshitaka Amano, whom Sakaguchi would later recruit to develop the visual style for Final Fantasy.

Eventually, Sakaguchi got his act together, graduated school, and entered Yokohama National University to study electronic communications. Unfortunately for his renewed interest in scholastic achievement, he quickly discovered video games. A classmate named Hiromichi Tanaka owned an Apple II, and their group of friends would stay up all night playing Western RPGs like *Wizardry* and *Ultima*. Sakaguchi didn't go in for arcade games, but these RPGs were something else: They had fantastic stories like the ones he devoured in the volumes of *Guin Saga*, and you could play them for hours on end. Which he did. Sakaguchi and his friends would pull all-nighters on Tanaka's Apple II. He battled monsters in *Ultima II* until he maxed out the amount of gold his character could carry, and the counter rolled over from 9999 back to 0.

Around 1983, during spring break of their third year at the university, Tanaka suggested they try taking part-time jobs at a new software publisher called Square that was looking for programmers. At the time, Square was a division of Den'yusha, a successful electrical contractor that laid power lines around Yokohama. The owner's son, Masafumi Miyamoto, saw an opportunity to make some serious money in the exploding computer game business. There was just one problem. "Miyamoto was quite enthusiastic about this business, but didn't know much about video games," Hisashi Suzuki, one of the first recruits and eventual CEO of Square, once said in an interview. "Imagine that such a person is your boss. It's bizarre. Sakaguchi was the only person who could say 'no' to Miyamoto because he had already demonstrated his leadership in technical terms."

Sakaguchi had learned his way around a computer, and parlayed his part-time job into a senior position at Square, producing graphical adventure games—like Infocom's text adventures, but with full-color, lightly-animated graphic scenes—for Japanese computer formats. Soon after, he dropped out of school for good.

Square's technical wizards were adept at pushing out beautiful graphics on the Japanese PCs at the time, and their games sold well—so much so that when Nintendo released its Family Computer game console in 1983, Square was uninterested in what it saw as a technical downgrade. "We thought of ourselves as the cutting edge of computer technologies," Suzuki said. "We ignored Famicom from the beginning... because we thought it was a toy." Eventually, as Famicom continued to grow in mainstream popularity and PC gaming stayed niche, Square had to shift its resources or die.

The company began by making up for lost time: Having largely ignored the Famicom during the first three years of its life, Square pumped out a whopping twelve games for the platform in the span of a single year, between December 1986 and December 1987. Many of these were developed by outside software houses and released in a big hurry. There were some minor successes but no breakout hits. It's no exaggeration to say that the future of the company was staked on a big game that Sakaguchi was putting together, to be released late that December, called *Final Fantasy*.

•

Although Nintendo had released the Famicom (redesigned and rechristened as the NES) in the US in late 1985, it was only a test-market release in New York City. The console didn't roll out nationwide until the spring of 1986, around the same time that a Famicom game was arriving in Japan that would change that country's video game scene forever: *Dragon Quest*.

Much like Square, the game publisher Enix was founded by an entrepreneur who knew nothing about making games. But whereas Masafumi Miyamoto started up a small studio by hiring developers, Enix's Yasuhiro Fukushima outsourced everything. Enix (a portmanteau of "ENIAC," an early model of computer, and "phoenix") placed advertisements in a variety of magazines in August 1982 announcing a game programming contest. It was a brilliant move. Hobbyist programmers around the country submitted their games to Enix, which cherry-picked the best ones and paid the winners their prizes in exchange for the rights to publish the games.

While Square was a boutique software house that only produced nine PC games between 1984 and 1987, Enix sprayed out "contest winners" like a firehose. In 1983, its first year as a publisher, it shipped 35 games for Japanese PCs. The games spanned genres—puzzles, adventures, shooters, even porn. Two big successes were *Door Door*, a puzzle game by a creator named Koichi Nakamura, and *The Portopia Serial Murder Incident*, an adventure game by Yuji Horii.

Enix ported both games to the Famicom when it moved into that business in 1985, and soon, Nakamura and Horii teamed up for the company's first original Famicom title. *Dragon Quest* made the role-playing game palatable to the millions of mainstream Famicom-owning consumers who were used to action and shooting games. It took the Dungeons & Dragons-inspired gameplay of computer RPGs and simplified it down to its barest essence, and Enix recruited popular manga artist Akira Toriyama—creator of *Dragon Ball*—to give the whole thing a familiar, friendly, rounded-off cartoon aesthetic.

Dragon Quest was an explosive hit, birthing a franchise that would soon rival Super Mario in popularity. It quickly inspired a slew of imitators, one of which was Sakaguchi's *Final Fantasy* in 1987. Sakaguchi decided that his game should follow the same basic concept of *Dragon Quest*—simplifying the RPG so that it could be played by casual players with a Famicom controller—but in most other ways he sought to distinguish it from Enix's massively popular game.

Where *Dragon Quest* had a single player-character, *Final Fantasy* players were asked to pick a team of four warriors, and were given the freedom to choose between six "jobs," which were patterned after Dungeons & Dragons character classes: Fighter, Thief, Monk ("Black Belt" in the original US version), Red Mage, White Mage, and Black Mage. You could choose these jobs in any configuration you liked, although some groupings were far more advantageous than others. While having a White Mage in the party to cast curative spells was certainly helpful, trying to get through the game with four of them would be extremely difficult. (But possible.)

You could also see your four characters on the screen, arrayed against each grouping of enemies. This gave the game's battles a distinctive look compared to *Dragon Quest*'s, which were shown from a first-person perspective. As in *Dragon Quest*, battles were conducted in a turn-based format in which the player entered in a command for each of the four characters, then watched the round of fighting play out automatically.

Sakaguchi didn't want round-faced manga characters on the game's cover. Instead, he turned to the artist whose work he had admired on the covers of *Guin Saga*, Yoshitaka Amano. His unique style, ethereal and delicate, was miles away from the simple cartoon characters of Toriyama, and made *Final Fantasy*'s packaging and marketing materials stand out on the shelves. Of course, it was also extremely difficult to translate these wispy illustrations into chunky pixel graphics. Even so, the *Final Fantasy* we see on the Famicom screen does resemble the feeling of Amano's work, evoking a lonelier, grimmer tone than *Dragon Quest*'s cheeriness. Sakaguchi and his compatriots may have considered Famicom a "toy," but they pushed hard to develop a more PC-like, adult aesthetic on Nintendo's platform, while still keeping the gameplay accessible.

Both series received bestselling sequels in rapid succession, and it didn't take long for Nintendo of America to see how popular RPGs were on Famicom. Attempting to replicate that phenomenon on NES, it took it upon itself to localize the first installments of both

Dragon Quest and Final Fantasy, releasing the games one after the other in 1989 and 1990 and promoting them heavily in *Nintendo Power* magazine. It actually devoted an entire issue to *Final Fantasy*, explaining every detail of the game to its two million subscribers in an attempt to woo players into experiencing the lengthy epic for themselves.

While Nintendo's full-court press surely created more than a few lifelong fans of what was quickly becoming known as the "JRPG," it wasn't quite enough. You can lead a horse to water, but you can't make him buy *Dragon Quest*. Nintendo was stuck with so many unsold copies of the US version (renamed *Dragon Warrior*) that it ended up giving the rest of them away for free with a $20 subscription to *Nintendo Power*.

For whatever reason, *Dragon Quest* didn't interest me, but I did want to play *Final Fantasy*. Not enough to ask for it for Christmas, but I'm pretty sure we found it at a yard sale not long after its initial release. I was eleven years old and I didn't understand it. I walked up to the first evil lord's castle where the princess was being held and he wiped me out in a split second. The concept of "grinding," fighting the same mobs of enemies over and over again to raise your characters' statistics, was foreign to me. I just thought the game was way too hard. Eventually I somehow bashed my way through that first castle, only to find even tougher challenges ahead. By the time I got to the Marsh Cave, where enemies poisoned you, sapping your health even faster, I gave up. I loved the *idea* of *Final Fantasy*, but this game made no sense to me. *Final Fantasy IV* came out for the Super Nintendo in 1991, and I ignored it.

The gateway drug, it turned out, was a SNES game called *Secret of Mana*, actually the second in a series called Seiken Densetsu in Japan. (The first, a Game Boy game, had been released here as *Final Fantasy Adventure*.) Produced by Sakaguchi's former classmate Hiromichi Tanaka, *Secret of Mana* combined RPG elements with action-oriented gameplay—a sort of cross between *Final Fantasy* and Nintendo's globally popular adventure game *The Legend of Zelda*. This combo meant that even grinding was fun, since I was swinging the sword myself and had that tactile satisfaction of landing a hit. *Mana* was also easier to make progress in, and up to three people could join in if you had the appropriate adapter and extra controllers. A middle school friend had *Secret of Mana*, and we'd all team up playing his copy. He also had *Final Fantasy IV*, and when he got bored with it, he sold it to me. Maybe, I thought, there was something to this RPG stuff after all.

Final Fantasy IV was nothing short of a revelation. While the original game certainly had some movie-like elements, this one was astonishingly cinematic: The opening, set to a dramatic musical score, faded in on a group of airships on a royal mission. In the half hour of exposition that followed, we met a cast of intriguing characters and saw their web of complex relationships, learned about the world, and were sent off on another mission, all before the first monster battle. The game was much less grindy than the first, and you could make extensive progress in the storyline without having to first wander around in a field killing Imps for hours. This was unlike any other video game I'd ever laid eyes on. I was a Square fan, and I was ready for whatever was next.

•

"We felt the rivalry from the Dragon Quest series," Sakaguchi begins, when I ask how *Final Fantasy V* came into being.

The first *Final Fantasy* had sold about half a million copies in Japan—solid numbers that allowed Square to stay in business, but about one-fifth of the sales of *Dragon Quest II*, which Enix had released earlier that year. *Final Fantasy II*, which Sakaguchi and company had completed in under one year, showed steady growth and sold over 750,000 copies. But *Dragon Quest III*, also released in 1988, sold a whopping 3.8 million copies, which no Famicom series but Mario had ever done or would ever do. Sakaguchi labored underneath the long,

long shadow of Dragon Quest. "Whatever we do, we have to one-up them," he thought.

The incredibly popular *Dragon Quest III* had allowed players to choose jobs, or classes, for their characters, as in the first *Final Fantasy*. But there was a twist: Once players leveled those characters up sufficiently, they could give them new jobs, reconfiguring their party mid-game. But class changes came at a high cost. For *Final Fantasy III*, Sakaguchi decided the best way to one-up Dragon Quest was to give players nearly unlimited freedom. The "job change" system he came up with let players switch their characters' classes on the fly at any time. "If you could become anything at any time in a game, what more could you ask for?" Sakaguchi says. "If you could become a Ninja in one battle and a White Mage in another, of course that's going to be fun." Boss monster weak against fire spells? Why, just change all of your characters into fire-casting Black Mages, and burn straight through him. It was a huge hit. *Final Fantasy III* sold twice as many copies as *Final Fantasy II*.

Final Fantasy IV didn't use the job change system. Instead, it featured a revolving cast of eleven playable characters who cycled in and out of your party at key moments during the story. This allowed Sakaguchi and his team to write a more intriguing and dramatic story, using the classes established in the previous games to give the characters personalities. Cecil, the main character, was a Dark Knight who overcame his circumstances to become a Paladin. The story wouldn't make sense if he could change into a Bard or a Black Mage whenever the fancy struck him.

For *Final Fantasy V*, Sakaguchi looked to combine the two previous entries in the series: The player characters wouldn't just be four generic randos as in *FF1* and *FF3*, but neither would those characters be defined by their respective professions. *Final Fantasy V* was going to one-up itself yet again. Not only would players again have the ability to reconfigure their parties' classes at any time, they'd also be able to carry over abilities from classes that they had played as for a while, thus creating mix-and-match characters with any combination of different abilities.

For example, a player could spend a few hours fighting as a White Mage. Experience points, or EXP, gained from monsters would boost that character's overall statistics—no matter what job they were using. But battles would now also grant ability points, ABP, which would boost only the level of whatever specific job they were using. A White Mage could use any White Magic in the game. But after gaining a few ABP, the character would learn a new ability called "White Magic Level 1." You could then change that character's job to Knight, then assign that Knight any one single ability from the list of skills you'd learned from spending time as other jobs. So you now had a sword-wielding damage dealer who could also use a Cure spell in a pinch.

Of course, there were always some downsides. The EXP each character gained set their basic stats (offense, defense, magic power, et cetera), and the jobs affected these base stats in different ways. A character assigned as a Knight would get big bumps to their physical offense and defense, but lose much of their magical power. So a Cure spell cast by a Knight would, as a rule, be less powerful than one cast by a true White Mage.

Not every job combination was useful. To take our Knight and White Mage as examples again, the Knight has an innate ability called Cover that allows him to automatically defend an imperiled friend by diving in front of them and absorbing physical damage for them. If you were to learn the Cover ability and equip it on a White Mage, who has extremely low physical defense and no ability to equip shields or heavy armor, you'd end up with a suicidal healer.

And then there were classes whose usefulness didn't make itself immediately apparent: Bard? Dancer? How were musicians going to help me defeat all these monsters? *Final Fantasy V* gave you the ability to do whatever you liked with its twenty different character classes, but left it to you to figure out how those seemingly disparate abilities might combine into a character stronger than the sum of their parts.

If all of these character classes were overwhelming to the player, they were even more overwhelming to the folks making the game. The task of translating Yoshitaka Amano's minutely detailed paintings into tiny pixel art went to Square's in-house artists, chief among them Kazuko Shibuya. As one of the only women on the Final Fantasy team—hell, as one of the only women making video games in the early 1990s—Shibuya was an integral part of the crew from its early days, joining in the pre-Famicom era and doing anime-style illustration for PC games like *Alpha* and *Cruise Chaser Blassty*.

It was Amano's art that defined Final Fantasy's marketing, but it was Shibuya's signature pixel art style that largely defined the contours of the game itself. And the decision to have five characters that could each wear the outfits of twenty different jobs meant tons of pixels had to be drawn. "There were two of us working on the jobs, but we had to do everything for them, including the designs. It was insanely difficult," Shibuya said in a 2013 interview. "I remember doing a magazine interview with Sakaguchi about *FF5* and saying, with some exasperation, 'There were too many damn jobs!!!'" Shibuya worked for a year straight simply drawing the main characters' battle artwork, she said.

"Yes, it was a lot of work," Sakaguchi says. "Yes, it was a lot of asset-making. Yes, it was a lot of data that we had to look at. But knowing that that was going to be the core feature, it was totally worth all that effort and figuring out how best to work the system, because at the end of the day, that was going to make it addictive."

•

For many players, including myself, the Final Fantasy trilogy on the Super Famicom represents the peak of the series. Hironobu Sakaguchi has one response, whenever an American fan tells him such a thing: "Why do you tell me now? You should have bought them back in the day, and voiced your opinion! It's kind of a weird feeling that people are saying that now. It wasn't something I expected to hear."

It was always a sticking point for Sakaguchi that his games, which sold millions of copies in Japan, couldn't get any traction outside his home country. Other Japanese-made games were flying off the shelves around the world now that Nintendo had released foreign versions of the Famicom. Nintendo's *The Legend of Zelda* wasn't quite an RPG, but it did have a lengthy quest and complex mechanics, and it was a big hit worldwide. Surely *Final Fantasy* could be, too. But that big break was slow in arriving.

The received wisdom was that RPGs were "too hard" for American console owners. If anything, though, RPGs were easier than action games. If you weren't good at

Super Mario Bros., you'd never beat it. But if you weren't good at *Final Fantasy*, you could eventually finish the game if you were persistent enough and patient enough to grind your characters' levels up to a point at which you could defeat all of the monsters. What RPGs were, if anything, was too complicated.

Square tried many tactics to get beginners acclimated to RPGs. The version of *Final Fantasy IV* that it brought to America stripped out some of the rules, options, and items that made the game more challenging and/or complicated. For example, there are a dozen different healing items in *Final Fantasy IV* with elaborate names like Gold Hairpin or Maiden's Kiss, each of which heals a different affliction. But in the American game, these are compressed into a single, inexpensive panacea item simply called Heal. (It also released a similar version in Japan as *Final Fantasy IV Easytype*.)

By all accounts, Square did initially intend on releasing *Final Fantasy V* in the US. It brought the game to the 1993 Consumer Electronics Show, and *Nintendo Power* reported multiple times, as late as its January 1994 issue, that the game was coming here with the title *Final Fantasy III*. But later that year, Square decided not to release the game—at least, not just yet. "I knew that this was a great game when I played early versions of it," said Ted Woolsey, a translator who joined Square in 1991, when I interviewed him for my first book *Power-Up*. "But the managers felt that the audience might not be ready."

"Instead," said Woolsey, "they felt we needed to grow the market in the US, and they pursued development of *Final Fantasy Mystic Quest*, which I helped write and translate." *Mystic Quest* was a sort of "RPG For Dummies" developed specifically for the US market. It eliminated anything that might cause players confusion: You couldn't roam freely around the world map, and were instead restricted to a set path. You didn't need to remember to equip new weapons and armor— everything new you found was instantly equipped (and always better than the last thing). If you lost a battle, there was no Game Over—you could just restart the battle and try again.

Square even released *Final Fantasy Mystic Quest* in Europe, which had precious few Square games (and console RPGs in general) at the time. If America seemed like an RPG-free wasteland to us, it surely looked like a Squaresoftian paradise to Europeans, who only got *Mystic Quest*, *Secret of Mana*, and the original *Seiken Densetsu* during the era when Square games were exclusive to Nintendo platforms.

I played *Mystic Quest* all the way through for the same reason a starving man wouldn't pass up stale bread and expired cheese. The graphics and music were up to Square's typical excellent quality standards, but the game itself was rather weak tea. *Mystic Quest* didn't succeed in its goal of making the series any more popular in any territory, and it wasn't what Square's existing fans wanted either.

Sakaguchi and the core Final Fantasy team had nothing to do with *Mystic Quest*, which was developed by a separate team in Osaka (and, like *Easytype*, was re-imported into Japan as *Final Fantasy USA*). Although he did yearn for a larger Western audience and took creative inspiration from Western fantasy and sci-fi, he says he wasn't consciously trying to design his games as global products. "It wasn't like these games were focused or centered around being successful in the West at all," he says. "But we did consider, from time to time, how do we make it so that maybe this could be a success outside Japan? Maybe we would have outside companies do some playtesting, make some reports or give some feedback. Some of the highlights were that the system was too complicated, the game itself was too complex, and the deformed [that is, big-head and cutesy] characters made it look like a kids' game. When you combined all these elements, the advice that we ended up getting from the Western market was no, this is not going to be appealing to the West. And they passed on it."

In a 1994 interview with a UK gaming magazine called *Super Play*, Woolsey elaborated on the decision:

"Although we're sure it's a great title, it hasn't been a hit with too many people in our focus groups," he said. "Although the more experienced gamers loved the complex character building, it's just not accessible to the average gamer."

Woolsey added that Square was "determined" to release it "once there's a larger audience," and that it tentatively planned to release the game as *Final Fantasy Extreme*, an attempt to turn the complicated nature of the job-change system into a selling point. But for now, it wasn't happening, and boy was I mad as hell.

•

In 1992, as Hironobu Sakaguchi and his team were hard at work on *Final Fantasy V*, I was hard at work on the sixth grade. It had become apparent to me that "video game reviewer" was a job that actual adults had, and this seemed like an excellent living. Play games and get paid for doing it? Get outta here. So I wrote my first couple of game reviews for the most prestigious publication that would have me: *The Scarlet Banner*, our sixth grade class newspaper.

Around the same time, a video game magazine aimed at older readers called *Video Games & Computer Entertainment* introduced me to the idea of fan-produced newsletters called "fanzines." The existence of fanzines stretches back to at least the science fiction fandoms of the 1930s, which I imagine had to be as isolating and weird as being a Square nerd in the early 1990s. In the pre-Twitter days, finding like-minded fans to share your obscure passions meant snail-mailing handwritten letters and Xeroxed amateur publications around the country. I named my fanzine *Video Zone*, after the final portion of the then-huge *Nick Arcade* television game show in which contestants went "inside a video game" courtesy of awkward blue screen technology. I reviewed games, shared news I found in America Online message boards, and wrote editorials about what a thirteen-year-old thinks of the business strategies of Nintendo, Sega, and others.

And in early 1994, once I found out Square was skipping over *Final Fantasy V*, I let loose a torrent of pubescent anger in one of these editorials. I've been telling you a lot about what thirteen-year-old Chris thought about things, but for now, I'd like to turn it over to the kid himself.

"I would like to scream in all caps about *Final Fantasy 5*," I began, not caring much for the niceties of Roman numerals. "Square USA takes so damn long to translate things, so they are skipping the Japanese *FF5* and only bringing over *FF6*. *Final Fantasy 6* is a masterpiece, I guess, and bringing out *FF5* would only delay *FF6*, which by the time it got over would be obsolete. The only reason they are skipping *FF5* is because they take too long to translate!"

The all-caps was coming.

"The other thing they do is take out pieces of the game so US players can beat it more easily, and taking out objectionable parts of the game! YOU STUPID PIECES OF $H!+! LEAVE THE DAMN GAME ALONE AND RELEASE IT!"

(Special Apology Section: I hereby apologize to any members of the 1994 Square localization team, and quite frankly to everyone who just read that last paragraph.)

Besides coming face-to-face with my tremendous capacity for taking things personally and lashing out with barely-censored expletives... and lack of regard for the nuances and difficulties of the video game business... and general self-destructive attitude... I do find it interesting that even at thirteen I was already aware that there was a complicated process involved in bringing a game from one country to another. I was gleaning a lot of this from editorials in those magazines aimed at older readers, which attempted to analyze and illuminate the inner workings of the game business in a way that *Nintendo Power* sought, if anything, to obscure. I was beginning to grasp that there were many different agendas at work, from the actual translation process to gameplay tweaking to dealing with the censorious content guidelines of Nintendo of America, which did its best to strip games of Satanic imagery, death, sexuality, alcohol, and anything else that was cool or awesome. If a Japanese game went unreleased in the West, it wasn't just a random occurrence. Someone, somewhere, had decided it.

Square did release *Final Fantasy VI* in the US that October—and yeah, it was a masterpiece, I guess. I knew I was getting it for Christmas that year when my dad said on a car trip, "We got you one of the games you wanted for Christmas. It cost *eighty bucks*." Bingo: No other game cost eighty bucks. It had a 24-megabit cartridge, which was *almost* as big as SNES cartridges ever got. The main cost driver of SNES game cartridges were the ROM chips, and as a producer of smaller print-run software Square didn't exactly have economy of scale on its side, so *Final Fantasy VI* rang in at the absolute high end of SNES game pricing.

But boy, was it worth every last one of my parents' dollars. Not only did *Final Fantasy VI* have the series's most complex and intriguing plotlines to date, with a cinematic presentation that made previous games look like a puppet show, but the graphics and sound quality were vast improvements over *Final Fantasy IV*'s. It was one of the most glorious things I'd ever seen on a game console. But *Final Fantasy VI* didn't satiate my desire for more Final Fantasy—it only amplified it. It soon became apparent that *Final Fantasy Extreme*, that promised out-of-order release of *FF5*, wasn't happening. I needed more, and if Square wasn't up to the task, it was time for Plan B.

•

Clearly, the only way I was going to permanently resolve the paucity of Japanese video games in my life was by going to Japan, maybe forever. I'd seen pictures, in gaming magazines, of a place called Akihabara. If these reports were telling the truth, then the city of Tokyo had an *entire district* devoted to video games. (In truth, Akihabara in those days was as full of radio equipment and home appliances as it was Famicom shops, but the image was true enough.) Did Japan also have, like, temples and stuff? Probably. But a *video game district*? Who would want to live anywhere else?

If going to Japan was the ultimate goal, it was unattainable for the moment. "Studying abroad" was a college thing, and that was a lifetime away. Glimpsing Japan through the small amount of translated material available was a start, but what if it was possible to go straight to the source? If I was willing to forego actually being able to read the dialogue in *Final Fantasy V*, then I should just be able to buy the Japanese version of the game. At least I'd be able to experience the music, the gameplay, and maybe get some of the story out of its puppet show... right?

For years, I'd been entranced by the back pages of magazines like *Electronic Gaming Monthly* and *Die Hard Game Fan*. Once I'd read all the news, reviews, and previews in the front, I could spend another hour poring over the classified ads in the back. This was where the import video game stores would list all of the Japanese games that you could buy from them at a premium price. *Die Hard Game Fan* itself was simply the publishing organ of a mail-order video game store of the same name in Tarzana, California. They'd devote full glossy pages to the latest import games that were never coming here, and of course the editorial opinion of this publication was that each of these games was the most amazing, mind-blowing orgasm of an experience since the last one. Supplies are limited! Call now!

So I did. One night in 1995 after school, I called Die Hard to inquire about the price of *Final Fantasy V*. The game had been out in Japan for almost three years—surely it would be heavily discounted by now! I got through to a store clerk and asked about the price.

One hundred and thirty dollars.

"Thanks," I said, and hung up. Plan B was looking like a failure.

•

It was a stroke of luck that buying a Japanese Super Famicom game was an option at all.

When Nintendo turned the Famicom into the Nintendo Entertainment System, it made many revisions to the hardware. Most significantly, it changed the shape of the game circuit boards. Famicom games plugged into the hardware by way of an edge connector that had 60 gold pins. NES cartridge connectors had 72 pins. So it was impossible to plug a Famicom game into an NES, at least, not without the aid of a converter device. These existed, but they represented an additional barrier. Fortunately, since both Japan and the US operated on the NTSC television standard, the games were perfectly compatible once the "region lock" was defeated. (European gamers, whose televisions used a different standard called PAL, were not so lucky.)

Super Famicom games wouldn't fit into a Super NES either, but it wasn't because the boards were different. In fact, the only obstacle was a pair of tiny plastic tabs inside the SNES's cartridge slot that did not exist in the Super Famicom. Super NES games had slots that the two tabs fit into while Super Famicom games did not. So all you had to do to "region-mod" your SNES was to take a pair of pliers and rip the tabs out.

In later years, Nintendo would region-lock its game systems like the Wii U and Nintendo 3DS with complicated software programs that only allowed games from one's home country to be played even if the physical cartridges were identical. But back then, defeating the region lock was as simple as ripping out a few extraneous pieces of plastic.

Or so I'd heard. Like the rumors of questionable origin I was discovering in newsgroups and reprinting in *Video Zone*, any piece of information one found on the internet was probably *more* likely to be total BS than true. So while I had reasonably deduced that I would be able to play this copy of *Final Fantasy V* when it came in, I didn't really *know*. The only way to test it was to buy a game and see what happened.

•

I'm not quite sure how I found GameLand. Did they advertise in *Electronic Gaming Monthly*? Did a knowledgeable netizen respond to a plea for help after my aborted phone call with Die Hard? The answer is lost to the ages. But somehow, I heard of another southern California game store that apparently had much better prices. Another quick phone call, and I found out that GameLand would sell me a copy of *Final Fantasy V* for $49.95 plus five bucks shipping. Now that was a reasonable birthday present that I could squeeze out of my parents. A follow-up phone call, a credit card number, and I was the owner of *Final Fantasy V*. In name, if not in physical fact just yet.

•

The manila bubble mailer took weeks to wend its way from Torrance, California to North Branford, Connecticut, truck to truck to truck, no real-time tracking available to chart its progress. Today, the arrival of a UPS truck is a daily occurrence in my life, barely something to notice. That one summer afternoon in 1995, the driver's knock at the door felt so momentous that I can remember it with utmost clarity.

As I opened the door to see the brown-uniformed driver holding that unassuming envelope containing The Lost Final Fantasy, asking for a signature, I was so filled with adrenaline that I froze up. *I can't sign this*, I thought! *I'm fifteen! It wouldn't be binding!*

"Okay!" I yelled out behind me, assuming my mom and dad would read my mind and know exactly what was going on. "Um!" My heart was beating rapidly. A terrifying thought flashed through my mind: What if my parents took too long getting to the door, and the driver left with the package? Fortunately, my dad arrived on the scene quickly to sign for thc package. The door shut. I sat down on the couch and ripped open the hand-addressed envelope with shaky hands.

I pulled out the Super Famicom cartridge. It was as I had seen in magazines: rounder, with a lighter-colored plastic. It seemed gentler, more graceful than the sharp angles of the American cartridges. And inside the envelope was an unexpected bonus—a folded-up *Final Fantasy V* poster, which I later discovered was actually the game's instruction manual. This deal was getting better and better! I looked up at my parents, sure they would join in with my elation.

"It's *used*," my dad said. Where I saw a minor miracle, he saw a loose cartridge and a dog-eared manual for which he'd just paid $55, which seemed too close to the price of a new game.

"It won't even fit in your machine!" my mom chimed in, eying its unfamiliar shape.

This was not going as well as I had hoped. "I know what I'm doing!" I said. But did I? I didn't really *know* if yanking out two pieces of plastic was going to let my SNES play Japanese games. Try to also put yourself in a 1995 state of mind here. The Super Nintendo was the family's primary video game console, the one for which we'd paid two hundred bucks a few years back. We were not rich people and that was not a small amount of money. My parents still occasionally played *Super Mario Kart* on it.

And here I was, proposing that I start ripping chunks out of it with a pair of pliers. Imagine a kid telling his parents in 2016 that he'd heard on the internet that if you jam a screwdriver into the disc slot of the PlayStation 4, it would play Xbox games.

"I think," said my dad, looking at everything, "those tabs are just there so you don't put the game in backwards." In his opinion, I was about to learn a very expensive lesson. Either way, the money was spent and the tabs looked like they'd be easy to pull out without damaging anything, so in went the pliers.

It wasn't as easy as the internet suggested. We really had to work at the tabs, twisting and turning, the nibs of plastic softening as we worked them. And they didn't come off cleanly—they left jagged remainders inside the formerly pristine cartridge slot. But they were gone enough that the Super Famicom cartridge fit in perfectly. All that was left was to turn on the power and cross my fingers.

The red LED light flickered on.
The screen remained black.
Silence.

無

mu

"nothingness"

Recently, as an experiment, I put a copy of *Final Fantasy V* into a Super Nintendo to note how long the screen stayed black before any graphics appeared. It wasn't more than a second or two, but it was a deliberate second, one I believe was put there intentionally by the designers. They wanted the first thing you saw to be a black screen that lingered for just a moment.

That day in 1995, all eternity passed in that second. My parents were right. I was wrong. I got duped.

Then: Lines of blue swiftly traced their way across the screen, painting what looked like the reflective surface of an ocean at midnight. From these colors, up rose the game's logo, gracefully, soundlessly, the shape of a dragon curled around the English words FINAL FANTASY V. But still, the silence. I was in thrall, and touched no buttons. What happened next was a hint of the sort of freewheeling fun that *Final Fantasy V* promised, a palate cleanser from its somber predecessor. An up-tempo melody kicked in, a few harp chords giving way to an upbeat horn section, trumpeting the beginning of a grand adventure.

The *Final Fantasy V* logo turned transparent, and behind its letters we could see the game's hero, Butz, riding his trusty chocobo steed Boco—a massive yellow flightless bird with a prominent beak—across a wide-open plain into unknown adventure.

As the boy and his bird made their way from letter to letter and the game's theme song played, a new wrinkle was added to this opening scene: The game's credits, the names of its creative team, began to appear, again in English, underneath the logo. Final Fantasy games had always had sequences crediting the creators, but none had ever appeared in such a dramatic fashion at the beginning of the game.

"That was intentional," Hironobu Sakaguchi would tell me later. "We wanted it to feel like you were going to go into a movie-like experience. It was less about getting our individual names out there, and more about taking you on a journey as if you were watching a movie."

Mission accomplished. And yet all of this would have impressed me a lot more had I not played *Final Fantasy VI* six months earlier, which pulled off a much more impressive introduction sequence, both technologically and aesthetically. I was experiencing *Final Fantasy V* not only out of place but, already, out of time.

The credits began with the Big Three: Sakaguchi, Yoshitaka Amano, and the game's longtime music composer Nobuo Uematsu, whose bright and bouncy composition was currently playing. These were people whose names I knew. The rest I did not. But looking at it today, it's a who's who of RPG legends. Tetsuya Takahashi, creator of *Xenoblade*, worked on the game's map graphics. Renowned creator of *Kingdom Hearts*

Tetsuya Nomura started here, drawing monsters. Yasunori Mitsuda, who would soon make a name for himself composing the score to Square's *Chrono Trigger*, was for now relegated to working on sound effects.

In fact, you can hear one of Mitsuda's contributions to *Final Fantasy V* just a few seconds after pressing the Start button. Another musical piece from Uematsu, this one somber, swells up as the parapets of a castle fade into view. We pan down to see, sitting atop the castle, a sleeping dragon. A robed human figure walks out from a door to stand next to the dragon, who awakens, stretches, and lets out an otherworldly, almost musical screech, a sound effect created by Mitsuda. (I'd find out later that he hated this job, and after *FF5*'s completion told his superiors that if they didn't let him compose a game, he'd quit. To their credit, Square agreed.)

So far, I was entranced by *Final Fantasy V*. That music! Those graphics! And topping it all off, everything I'd seen so far had either been in English or dragon-speak. Maybe this wasn't going to be so hard after all! Now a girl in pink hair emerges from the same door, walks up to the other character, and for the first time, the familiar blue-and-white Final Fantasy text box appears on the screen, with the game's first line of dialogue.

レナ 「お父様！

A simple pair of words that any Japanese kid or first-year Japanese language student would be able to read. But to me at that moment there wasn't a single decipherable thing in there besides an exclamation point. Start a game of *Final Fantasy V* in English today, and you'll see this line in translation:

Lenna: Father!

But even in this single-word line of dialogue, there's already something lost in translation: In Japanese, Lenna had said *otō-sama* instead of *otō-san*, using a higher level of honorific title. So that indicates to us that Lenna and her dad are probably royalty. In English, we lose that. Compounding the problem is that in this simple act of translating a two-word line, we've nearly doubled the size of the text from seven characters in Japanese to thirteen in English. Those extra characters have to go *somewhere*—but it's likely that the *Final Fantasy* team has already packed the expensive, precious ROM space on the cartridge near to full with data. Where do they go? This was the impossible task of the Super Famicom translator, like Ted Woolsey, trying to cram English into a space that only fit Japanese. It was about making hard cuts.

More relevant to me at the time, even this tiny amount of text added worlds of meaning I wasn't getting. I didn't know that character's name was Lenna. I didn't know the other character was her father—I didn't even know that character was a *man*, with his amorphous purple robes and headgear. I was right to be confident that I could get *Final Fantasy V* running, but I shouldn't have been so confident that I'd be able to play it alone.

•

The main character of *Final Fantasy V* is named Butz. Pronounced "Butts." Don't giggle: America has our share of famous Butzes, including NFL linebacker Dave Butz and two-time Tony award winner Norbert Butz. Still, even with so many proud carriers of the name Butz, all official English-translated versions of the game render this character's name as "Bartz." Ironically, there's a game series that changed a character's name *to* Butz in the English version—*Phoenix Wright: Ace Attorney*. The original version had punny Japanese names for all of the characters, so in the English translation, Capcom changed the name of the doofus "Yahari Masashi" to "Larry Butz." His motto: "When something smells, it's usually the Butz."

Here's another strange fact: Simply going off of the game data of the original Super Famicom version of *Final Fantasy V*, the main character *has no name at all*. In all of the screenshots in the instructions, the character is given the placeholder name of "Square."

None of the game's characters are mentioned by name in the manual. And when you first meet Butz, you're asked to fill in his name. No default name is set in the game's program.

So how do we know it's the Butz? Well, if you look carefully at the screenshot on the back of the game's *box*, you can see the Japanese version of his name in a battle scene. But you could also find this information and much more in *Final Fantasy V Basic Knowledge*, the first part of the game's three-volume strategy guide, released in Japan on November 20, 1992, a few weeks before the game itself. This small-format paperback is less of a spoilery walkthrough and more of a primer on the game you were about to play, full of character backstories, gorgeous Yoshitaka Amano watercolors, and basic tutorials that the game manual itself was just too small to handle. And at just 534 yen, about $5, it was almost a piece of promotional material for the game: Buy it and read through it to see if you want to spend the 9,800 yen (about $100) on the game itself. (Super Famicom games were as a general rule much more expensive in Japan than in the US.)

From *Basic Knowledge*, we learn that our four starting characters have full names, which are spelled out in English in the book: Butz Klauser, Lenna Charlotte Tycoon, Galuf Doe, and Faris Scherwiz. The "Doe" here, used like the name "John Doe" in the US court system, illustrates that Galuf has lost his memory and doesn't remember his full name. Eventually, it's revealed that Galuf is actually a king, and his full name is Galuf Halm Baldesion. None of these last names appear in the game (except for Tycoon, but only as the name of the kingdom in which Lenna and her father live). They have no gameplay reason to exist. The Final Fantasy team just loved building out these intricate fantasy worlds, even if the details they imagine don't explicitly make it into the game itself.

Faris is probably the most interesting of the game's playable characters. You're meant to believe that Faris, the gruff-talking captain of a pirate ship, is a man. She's not. Before you find out the truth, there's a scene in which she falls asleep in an inn, and Butz and Galuf, suspicious of this mysterious captain with whom their group has made an uneasy alliance, sneak into the room and look at her while she sleeps. They come out with little heart icons over their heads and flushed expressions on their tiny pixel-faces. It's only later that Galuf calls Faris out, and she admits to posing as a man to keep her pirate crew in line.

Note that if you don't read Japanese, you understand absolutely none of this, and are liable to come away with the perfectly reasonable conclusion that Bartz and Galuf are both attracted to dudes.

The woman who poses as a man to join a pirate crew, army, or some other boys' club is an old trope in folklore around the world. When I ask Sakaguchi about it, his first response is that they were probably thinking about *Ribon no Kishi* ("Ribbon Knight," localized here as *Princess Knight*), the popular manga by Osamu Tezuka with a similarly disguised heroine. "She was my character that I came up with," he says, staking his creative claim. But Sakaguchi is always quick to note that he wasn't the only one coming up with the story.

•

Sakaguchi always had a writing partner. For the first three Final Fantasy games, he worked with outside collaborator Kenji Terada, who had written scripts for popular anime series like *Kinnikuman* and *Dirty Pair*. By *Final Fantasy V*, with more successes behind him and more talent on the bench, he looked in-house. Yoshinori Kitase, who had worked on *Final Fantasy Adventure* and *Romancing SaGa*, was a newcomer to the *Final Fantasy* team but Sakaguchi made him his right-hand man. The writing process, Sakaguchi says, was a team effort.

"In terms of story writing, I handled everything up through *Final Fantasy VI*," he tells me. "But when I say that I wrote the story, it's really closer to a plot... I laid the groundwork, and I had key moments, key lines that really were meaningful and critical to those scenes. But one approach that we were taking differently is, starting with *FF3*, we realized that because we had to work with our programmers to make these scenes happen and come alive, if we had given them every little detail of instruction, it became a little difficult to work that way. We wanted them to have a bit of a part, and take some work into their own hands as well." If it turned out that some of Sakaguchi's pre-written dialogue just wouldn't work in the scene that was transpiring, he says he was alright with throwing it out: "We were free-form in that way."

The actual scripting was a back-and-forth improvisation between Sakaguchi and Kitase. "I would take over maybe the first three scenes, and write the overview and the key moments," Sakaguchi says. "And then I would toss the next three scenes over to Kitase. And then it would get handed back to me."

Sakaguchi says that during this era, he was still getting down to the nitty-gritty of planning, plotting out for the programmers exactly how many squares a character would walk, what expression would be on their face, where the treasure chests would be placed in the dungeons. "There was kind of a nice rivalry between Kitase and myself," he says. "The daily ritual was, we'd show up at work, and I would have worked on something, and Kitase would have too. You know when you have those moments: One, two, three, show what you did? We'd see each other's work, and I'd be like, oh, that's actually not bad."

"But Kitase played some dirty tricks on me," Sakaguchi says. "Like the Kobayashi Maru."

In the movie *Star Trek II: The Wrath of Khan*, the Kobayashi Maru is a simulated rescue mission given to would-be Starfleet captains. The simulation is impossible to win and usually results in the deaths of the crew—it is simply meant to test a cadet's reactions to a no-win situation. Captain James T. Kirk, played by William Shatner, defeats the test by reprogramming the computer simulation the night before, allowing him to come away victorious, confounding his superiors.

Sometimes, Kitase would show up in the morning with an idea for a lavish, spectacular scene he wanted to write into *Final Fantasy V*. Perhaps he wanted all of the characters to fall off a cliff after a dramatic showdown. "There's no way we can do this," Sakaguchi would say. The program wouldn't be able to handle it. And yet, Kitase had done it.

"Well, last night, after you left the office, I had our programmers write a special program for me..." Kitase would respond. He'd gone behind the boss's back and had the programmers hack in his "impossible" concept, pulling a Captain Kirk.

"I admit that Kitase is probably better at coming up with spectacle," Sakaguchi says. So what, I asked him, did you do to counter that?

"Usually the more dramatic, moodier scenes," he says. "In order for me to have my moment, I wanted to make players cry."

Hearing this, I recalled an early scene in *Final Fantasy V*, when the party climbs up a mountain to search for Lenna's dragon. As you're moving through its plateaus and caverns, you start to see that the mountain is dotted with flowery purple bushes you've never seen before. But if you walk into one, there's a distorted effect on the screen and an unpleasant buzzing sound. If you check your status menu, you'll see that all of your characters are now inflicted with Poison, which saps hit points over time. You have to cure them all with Antidote items, or with curative spells, and then assiduously avoid stepping on any more purple bushes.

At the climactic scene of this dungeon, Lenna finds her dragon in a rough state, but sees, as we do, that the healing herbs on this mountain are behind a giant patch of poison shrubs. So she selflessly and agonizingly walks, while the screen buzzes and distorts, through the bushes and back with the herbs, then collapses. It's a brilliant bit of using a gameplay feature to foreshadow and explain a storyline sequence that wouldn't ordinarily make sense. And maybe even make a few players cry. That scene, Sakaguchi told me, was indeed one of his.

•

"I like telling this story because it's true, and no one believes it," Andrew Vestal says. "I did a search for 'Final Fantasy' and there were no pages on the internet. So I decided I was going to make a website for Final Fantasy."

It was the spring of 1995, and the internet was going mainstream. America Online, the service through which many Americans (including me) connected to the net, added the World Wide Web to its list of offerings in May. Amazon.com opened for business in July. Match.com went into live beta. eBay launched in September. But for me, there was just one destination: The UnOfficial Squaresoft Home Page. Only one other guy in my high school was also into Final Fantasy, and two nerds talking about White Mages over lunch does not a subculture make. The internet let all of the likeminded Square junkies find each other, and Andrew Vestal, in Dallas, Texas, was our fifteen-year-old king.

Andrew was my age, but had been an early bloomer in regards to *Final Fantasy*. He got the first game as a Christmas gift the year of its release, and played the hell out of it. Once he finished it with a party of two White Mages and two Black Mages, no easy task, just to prove he could. When *Final Fantasy IV* came out, he estimates that he played it at least a dozen times. "In my defense," he adds, "it's only like 20 to 30 hours long. It's actually quite zippy." I didn't ask how much time he put into *Final Fantasy VI.* But in the months following its release, he dedicated his free time to building the first website devoted to Square.

His mission was nothing short of 100 percent completion: Amass every single bit of information about Square on the internet. Fortunately for his sanity and his single megabyte of storage, there wasn't much to be amassed: some fan-created MIDI files of the games' soundtracks, some extremely low-resolution screenshots, and text files called FAQs (which in this case were generally not actual lists of "Frequently Asked Questions," but game walkthroughs). The UOSHP served to both collect the information about Square's games online and amplify it by encouraging fans to find and create more.

Andrew had also imported a copy of *Final Fantasy V* that summer. "I still remember this real sense of unreality," he says of booting up the game for the first time. "You know those science fiction short stories about how a book or a movie or an album slips through from a parallel universe, where things went a little bit differently? It felt like that, in real life. Like something that did not exist."

"There's something really primal and awesome about ripping the tabs out of your Super Nintendo," he said. "It's the world's most simple physical region locking, but the fact that it's so simply and violently circumvented made it a strong part of the experience of playing that game."

We also shared the experience of not being able to read it. The only Japanese-language resource I had was the instruction manual to *Mario Paint*, a mouse-based painting tool/game for the SNES that for whatever reason still had Japanese characters in its array of "stamps" that players could use to draw and create with. The manual gave a basic rundown of the reading of these characters, and so for a while I was using it (and my previous knowledge of the Final Fantasy series) to decipher the names of the items that I was picking up during my adventure.

The first word I ever read in Japanese was "potion," the first item I picked up in the game. The first words Andrew Vestal ever read in Japanese, at around the same time, were "yes," "no," and "tent," another classic Final Fantasy item. "*Te-n-to*," he said, sounding out the three kana syllables used to approximate the English word. "*Te-n-to*. Tento. Tent! It's a tent!"

We, the few who had imported *Final Fantasy V* without being able to read it, were making a bit of progress in our individual studies. But what we all needed was an expert. Poking around America Online,

I somehow made the acquaintance of Nora Stevens. Since we both had AOL accounts, I'm going to guess that I emailed her after seeing her post on a Final Fantasy newsgroup. At the time, Nora was eighteen and a freshman at the University of Michigan. While still in high school she'd spent some time on a homestay in Japan, where she picked up some Japanese Final Fantasy games. She'd only had *Final Fantasy V* for a year or so, and wasn't that far along in her Japanese language studies, but that made her the closest thing to an expert I could find.

This internet thing was working out amazingly well. I had a *cool older friend*. A girl! Who was in college! And played Final Fantasy games in Japanese! She introduced me to an online acquaintance of hers, a Japanese fan named Tatsushi Nakao, who was currently finishing up a degree at the University of Colorado Boulder. He'd created another early Final Fantasy fan page, with a twist: He called it "Illucia, the Town of Final Fantasy," and it was an elaborate graphically-oriented site that looked like an RPG town, with different buildings that you'd click on to find more information about the games. Tat, as he went by for short, grew up in Japan and was quite familiar with *Final Fantasy V*, and even had a bunch of Japanese-language strategy guides that he could refer to.

Somehow, I convinced Nora and Tat that we should create a *Final Fantasy V* FAQ, which didn't exist anywhere on the internet at that point. And which I sorely needed. Nora would create tables of all of the abilities, items, and skills in the game, Tat would write the walkthrough, and I'd pull it all together into a formatted file. And here's where we really decided to go nuts: The FAQ would actually be bilingual, showing the Japanese text that appeared in the game next to an English translation, thus giving the English-speaking world the tools they needed to poke their way through.

And as Tat was sending pieces of the walkthrough, I'd use them to make my way through the game. I didn't mind if nobody else used this FAQ, but at the same time, it was thrilling to imagine that we'd help more and more people play the One That Got Away.

•

"Zippy," as Andrew Vestal described *Final Fantasy IV*, is also a great adjective to describe *Final Fantasy V*. The layers of abstraction that are necessary in 16-bit game design are all part of the appeal of classic RPGs. Your character on the map screen is the same size as the entire town he just entered. The town scales up when you enter it relative to your character's size, but it's still not proportional: You can run down the streets of that town in about two or three seconds. As you blaze through the game, you never spend too much time in any one location or storyline. As game machines became more powerful, designers looked to craft RPG worlds that emphasized realistic scale. In today's games, a skyscraper towers over a human being, and an empty hallway takes as long to navigate in the game as it would in real life. This makes games less abstract, but it can also make them more boring. *Final Fantasy V*, by contrast, is 30 of the quickest hours you'll ever spend in an RPG.

The reason that the King of Tycoon leaves Lenna and sets off on his journey in the game's opening scene is because the wind has stopped blowing, an indication that something is wrong with the Wind Crystal. Once your merry band of warriors is assembled, you shove off for the Shrine of the Wind, the residence of the Crystal and the game's inaugural "dungeon"—a term that in RPGs refers to any locale filled with enemies and treasures, regardless of whether it takes place underground, above ground, in the sky, et cetera. At this point, you don't have any "jobs" at all—all of your characters are marked as *suppin*, or "bare," meaning they can use nothing except simple physical attacks and items. You play this first dungeon with these basic characters, which gives you a chance to learn the ins and outs of the turn-based fighting system before you have to worry about jobs.

That comes rather quickly. The Wind Crystal has somehow shattered into pieces, which is very bad because as far as anybody knows, these four ancient crystals are the only things holding the world together. Silver lining: Each shattered piece of crystal turns out to contain the "soul of a warrior"—that is, a new job for you to try on. At the end of the shrine, you acquire six jobs: Knight, Monk, Thief, White Mage (called "Priest" in the strategy guide, which lists English-language versions of most of the game's class, place, and character names), Black Mage (called "Wizard"), and Blue Mage. Suddenly, you're dumped back out into the world map, and you've got to make a decision, just like at the beginning of the original *Final Fantasy*: You have six jobs and only four characters. What do you want to do? It's all up to you. Knight/Monk/White Mage/Black Mage would be a decent party, with lots of physical attack strength (which in the case of the bare-fisted Monk doesn't require you to buy expensive weapons) and the ability to attack and heal with magic. But the Thief lets you steal items from enemies. And the Blue Mage lets you learn magic spells from enemies, which can be very powerful—and extremely useful in specific situations.

You're going to have to make a choice. Fortunately, it's not permanent. As you begin to fight battles and gain the AP that let you level up the jobs and learn new techniques, you might even want to start switching jobs. After you fight just ten battles, a character who has been playing as a White Mage will learn the skill "White Magic Level 1." You can now switch this character to a Black Mage and add that skill to their battle menu, giving you a character who can cast every Black spell you've acquired so far, as well as the three weakest White spells. (And that's okay because at this point in the game you only have access to the three weakest White spells anyway.) So already you can experiment with mixing and matching, although at this point your best bet is to keep reconfiguring your party on an ad hoc basis.

It gets much more confusing. The Water Crystal isn't far away, and it too shatters mysteriously, further imperiling the world but giving you even more jobs: Time Sorcerer, Magic Swordsman ("Enchanter" in the strategy guide), Summoner, Berserker, and Red Wizard. Now you're asked to weigh many alternatives. Red Wizard is tempting but ultimately crap: They can use both White and Black magic right out of the box—but only up to level 3. Summoner lets you call down magical creatures to kick ass for you, but these are generally fairly MP-intensive spells, making the job kind of useless unless you're in a boss fight. The Berserker can't be controlled—they simply attack with vastly increased power every turn.

So many choices, so quickly! But the genius of *Final Fantasy V* is that there is no "right" way to tackle its challenges. While there are certainly exploitative tactics you can use in most major battles, the game doesn't throw too many roadblocks in front of you that force you to always create the "perfect" party for a given situation. You can just get out there, have fun, and bash your way through with whichever specialties you like. But to really understand *Final Fantasy V*—to truly plumb its surprising depths—you've got to learn the subtleties of all its jobs.

•

Fighting through more dungeons and adventures, your party eventually reaches the castle of Karnak, where the Fire Crystal (surprise) ends up shattering as well. Things are not going so well for these crystals! This dungeon is a bit more hairy for you than the last one because the castle that was (unadvisedly) sucking all the power out of the Fire Crystal is now on fire and about to explode. And you're in its basement. A timer appears on the lower right corner of the screen. You've got ten minutes to get the hell out of there.

Final Fantasy V was the first game in the series to feature these timed sequences in which you end up with a Game Over if you don't move fast. Suddenly, the lackadaisical, wait-your-turn role-playing game turns into a nail-biting thriller. Are you used to leisurely scrolling through menus to find just the right spell? Better get a lot faster!

"Our programmer came up with the idea," says Sakaguchi, "and Kitase and I started messing around with it." Playing Final Fantasy on a timer was fun, the designers found. Too fun. "We got way too addicted to it," he says. The ability to create intricate, strictly timed events was like lighter fluid on the fire of Sakaguchi and Kitase's friendly creative rivalry. Sakaguchi would create an elaborate sequence and challenge Kitase to complete it in three minutes. Kitase would respond by creating a two-minute challenge for Sakaguchi.

What they discovered was fun about the timer wasn't simply about challenging the player to keep their thumb on the B button to dash quickly, or to scroll through menus more efficiently. The timers could be used to build elaborate risk-reward sequences. In the case of Karnak, the castle is full of rare, enticing treasures guarded by monsters. There's a dagger called the Main Gauche, which does little damage but lets the wielder automatically evade 25 percent of all physical attacks: great for your mages who don't attack often. There's the healing spell Esuna, which cures all afflictions. There's a Ribbon, the most powerful headgear in the game.

You want all this stuff? Yes, you do. But your first time through Karnak, your greed will probably end in your death. Even if you make it all the way through, a boss fight stands in your way. And of course, you're even encouraged to slow your roll during this boss fight, because the boss can use a powerful spell called Death Claw that you can learn if you've brought a Blue Mage along. Death Claw reduces an enemy's hit points to almost nothing while leaving them paralyzed. It's useful as hell. You want this, too.

So while it's quite easy to run out of the castle and avoid the automatic Game Over, the rewards for trying to pull off a perfect Karnak run are too sweet to pass up. This is a difficult challenge for the newbie *FF5* player, and a good (if ultimately optional) check-in on your understanding of the jobs and abilities at your disposal. There's another optional timed challenge later in the game in which you infiltrate an underwater dungeon with only a few minutes of air supply in an attempt to get one final powerful job class. But had Sakaguchi and Kitase not had so much restraint, the game might have been full of these challenges, and worse off as a result.

"As we were playing it, we noticed that we were getting hooked on it," Sakaguchi says. "But after being hooked on it for so long, we realized this can't be switched on at all times. The basic rule was that we'd have to limit the usage of it, only use it when it was meaningful, and it would bring the tension across to the players as well."

In later games in the series, Sakaguchi and crew would use the timers to great effect. *Final Fantasy VI* uses them in the classic opera scene, regarded as one of the series's most thrilling sequences, as well as in the dramatic escape from the Floating Continent. *Final Fantasy VII* uses one early on when the party blows up the Mako Reactor, and at various other points, including a tragic flashback that uses a countdown timer that always ends in failure. Any Final Fantasy player knows that when a little timer appears onscreen, it's time to haul ass.

•

As players, sometimes we don't really understand why we enjoy games.

We *think* we do. Growing up and reading about Nintendo's game design genius Shigeru Miyamoto, creator of the Zelda and Super Mario games, we read these flowery descriptions of the "magical, inventive, mysterious worlds" and "memorable characters" that came from the mind of this shaggy-haired, banjo-picking daydreamer with the goofy grin. The Mushroom Kingdom! The pig-demon, Ganon! And we internalize this: These storytelling elements, these must be the secrets to Miyamoto's success.

The first time I ever sat down to interview Miyamoto, for my first book *Power-Up*, I asked him about his stories, his characters, where they come from, how he came up with these designs that became so well known worldwide. It came as a shock when he put the brakes on that line of questioning almost immediately. His job wasn't to come up with fanciful stories, he said. His job was better described as *ningen kōgaku*—"human engineering." We like Miyamoto's stories because the gameplay is so expertly engineered, but we don't notice how well designed the games are. Like all good design, it disappears. We remember the adventure.

I didn't get to speak to Sakaguchi for *Power-Up*, but it's quite likely that if I had, he might have smashed my assumptions in a similar way. In our 2016 interview, we'd just finished up talking about the *Final Fantasy VI* opera sequence when he interjected with a point he didn't want to be ignored.

"A lot of times, people talk about story and characters, and we want to get really deep into that, which is fine," he said. "But one very critical theme that should not be left out from talking about Final Fantasy is... planning out the world and the map, and how it all works, and how it dovetails into the progression of the story."

At this, Sakaguchi took a piece of paper and started quickly sketching out a sample map of a Final Fantasy game. "You would first start out on probably the smallest island. In order for you to journey on to the next land, we would talk about transportation vehicles. So whether it was a ship, or the airship, or a chocobo, there was something you were going to have to get in order to move to the next place."

Chocobos, tall emu-like birds, are the horses of the Final Fantasy worlds, and obtaining one is always a treat. Not only are they darned cute, but they allow you to quickly dash across the world map without getting into any enemy encounters, thus freeing you up to explore more of the continents at your leisure. Perhaps most importantly, riding on a chocobo is always accompanied by the familiar, jaunty "Chocobo Theme" from composer Nobuo Uematsu, one of the only musical motifs repeated throughout the series. You begin *Final Fantasy V* with a chocobo, Butz's loyal companion Boco, and soon after you get Faris's pirate ship to sail off the continent.

"But then," Sakaguchi says, "once you get to the next place—let's say you got the ship, and it looks like you can get there with the ship, but you can't because there's all these cliffs. And you realize you need an airship. And then there's another piece of land, but there's some sort of magical power bordering it." He scribbles a "magical barrier" around a continent.

Once Lenna daringly rescues her flying dragon from the poisonous plants, you can fly around the world, although your dragon is still impeded by tall mountains. But every Final Fantasy player knows the real *ne plus ultra* of transit: The airship. Since the first game, finding an airship has meant freedom, full mastery of the world, the ability to circumnavigate the globe. The Super Nintendo games use a fun graphical trick to enhance that feeling of wind-in-your-hair liberation. The SNES hardware has a feature called "Mode 7" that allows the game to arbitrarily skew, rotate, and scale a 2D bitmap in order to pull off a faux 3D effect. *Final Fantasy V* makes scant use of this, but when you get into the airship, the ground bends away from you, giving a sort of curvature-of-the-earth effect, sending an unmistakable visual message that you are now free to move about the planet.

"The thing that players then most appreciate," Sakaguchi continues, "is that once you journey through, you can always go back to where you came from." And at that point, he said, the designers made sure that the various townspeople you visited at the start acknowledge the journey you've been on: "'How did you get over that magical wall border?' That was very time-consuming, but that appreciation was probably necessary. There's a lot of focus on narrative, story, characters. But that's really only half of it. The other half is planting these little intricate details. Maybe it's the treasure box that didn't open."

Final Fantasy games are film-like stories, but they are also intricately designed puzzles, ones that Sakaguchi is particularly proud of designing. The interplay between the linear narrative, the puzzles, and the non-linear exploration is what leaves us, Sakaguchi says, with the impression that a Final Fantasy game had a memorable story.

"A blend of both is what makes it," he says.

•

Feeling the wind in your hair, you're rocketing across a skewed bitmap in your airship, master of all that lies beneath you, and maybe you get to thinking: *Isn't this world a little... small?*

Granted, the world is never quite as small as it seems in a Final Fantasy game. Once you've explored the continents of *Final Fantasy IV*, for example, you still have to travel beneath the earth into the underworld, a lava-filled subterranean paradise for dwarves, then finish the game on the surface of the moon. But the planet's surface is still the largest part of the explorable space in the game. If you come in to *Final Fantasy V* having just played its immediate predecessor, you might be thinking it's getting a little bit cramped on that map screen.

Why the small map? Well, to talk about that we need to do a quick rundown of the story so far. The short, short version: A meteor lands on the planet. It contains

Galuf, who loses his memory on impact, but joins your party along with Lenna at the game's onset. A second meteor falls. It contains a strangely-dressed soldier, who addresses Galuf as "my lord," then dies. Later, the party discovers a third meteor, and finds out that its rider was a werewolf, who *also* knows Galuf, but *also* dies before they can get the story out of him.

Unlike the random "Light Warriors" of the first *Final Fantasy*, the characters of *Final Fantasy V* are all residents of this world. Lenna (and Faris, it later turns out) are from the kingdom of Tycoon. Butz, the wanderer, was born in a remote town tucked in the northern mountains called Lix, which you can visit once you get the airship. But… where's Galuf from?

Finally, Galuf regains his memory: He's an alien from outer space! And more specifically, he journeyed here from his home planet to stop the return of an evil wizard known as Exdeath. It turns out that, prior to the events of this game, Galuf and three of his best pals had had a little Final Fantasy adventure of their own that culminated in them fighting Exdeath and sealing him away, using the four elemental crystals on another planet. This planet. Turns out that even though those crystals give you that sweet, sweet job candy when they shatter, they're also the only thing imprisoning the universe's biggest a-hole.

Final Fantasy V's story is often criticized as being shallow, and compared to the games that bookend it, that is undeniably true. There's very little character development to speak of, no gray areas between good and evil, no love stories, and really not that much meaningful interaction between... well, anybody. The party groups up, bops around the world, discovers a big bad so one-dimensional that his name literally has the word "death" in it, and sends him packing.

I suspect this is a side effect of the game's fundamental design principles. Consider: Who is Cecil in *Final Fantasy IV*? A Dark Knight who becomes a Paladin. Who is Locke in *Final Fantasy VI*? A Thief who insists on being referred to as a "treasure hunter" instead. Strago is a Blue Mage, Sabin is a Monk. Each character's backstory and personality stem from their job distinctions. What one does for a living, one's special talents—these are precisely the things we might start inventing if we were fleshing out fictional characters. And these are precisely the things that Sakaguchi and Kitase could *not* attribute to any of *Final Fantasy V*'s characters because those characters must be able to change from a Bard to a Knight to a Red Mage at any moment. No wonder they're such boring nobodies.

But even this is not necessarily a weakness. "At the time, there was disappointment that the story was so much simpler to the twisting narratives of *FF4* and

FF6. But nowadays I feel like that's a strength because it doesn't get bogged down in a lot of dumb melodrama that I don't care about," Andrew Vestal says. "It's because the story is so dumb that I can slip back into that world so easily. I can just tune it out."

There is no twist ending to the first act. The story proceeds exactly how you'd expect: The Earth Crystal, the last line of defense, shatters. Exdeath escapes and leaves for his (and Galuf's) home world. Galuf's granddaughter Krile arrives on the final meteor to take Galuf back home. The party waves goodbye, but ultimately decides they can't abandon the fight. So they figure out how to open up a one-way gate to join Galuf, leaving their hometowns behind, on their way to another world.

WORLD 2

"WHY WASN'T I BORN IN JAPAN? Americans are so uncool. I want to become Japanese."

Wandering around the convention center at Penn State University, Toshio Okada heard variations on this phrase time and again. It was the summer of 1995, and Okada had flown out from Tokyo to attend the second annual Otakon, one of the earliest US fan conventions devoted to Japanese manga and anime. The inaugural Otakon had featured no Japanese guests. Okada was the first, and he was a huge get for the then-tiny convention of only 450 attendees: He was the co-founder of the popular animation studio Gainax, which was just a month away from premiering the first episode of its new TV anime *Neon Genesis Evangelion*.

On returning to Japan, he quickly penned an account of his Otakon experience for the weekly magazine insert of the *Asahi Shimbun* newspaper, titled "Anime Culture Is Super-Cool!: The American Otaku Who Love Japan." He began by quoting an anonymous American young person who lamented his own non-Japaneseness, and went on to marvel at how the American fans of Japanese cartoons were importing words like *otaku* (geek) and *dōjinshi* (fanzine) untranslated, creating elaborate costumes of anime characters, and learning Japanese (Otakon featured a language workshop).

Much as the word "geek" began as a pejorative before being embraced by that community, so too did "otaku" get its start in the 1980s as a derogatory word for obsessive and socially awkward fans of pop culture. But in the usage of the American Otakon attendees, it simply meant "a fan of Japanese pop culture."

This semantic gulf has probably resulted in more than a few cultural snafus. It certainly did in my case. Although Japan seemed so far away that summer of 1995, college application time arrived fairly quickly. I chose Tufts University, outside of Boston, primarily because it had an extensive Japanese program and a partnership with Kanazawa University in Japan. I spent my entire junior year there on a study-abroad program, starting in the fall of 2000. Early that year, while a Japanese student at the university was telling me about all the games she was currently playing, I responded, "Ah, so you're an otaku, then."

Her face froze up. As did her friend's. "We don't really say that," she said. She'd describe herself as "*gēmu-suki*," she said—"enjoys games." And the implication was that I probably should use that phrase, too, unless I wanted people to think I was...

Was what? Okada had noted the "negative implications" of the word in Japan. How bad was it? About this bad: In

1989, Tokyo police arrested Tsutomu Miyazaki, a serial killer who had murdered four girls between the ages of four and seven. Miyazaki was found to own a collection of over 5,000 VHS tapes, including some anime. For this, the media dubbed him the Otaku Murderer.

What's more, as Okada was penning his Otakon story in the *Asahi*, Japan was still reeling from the terrorist attacks on its subway system in March 1995. A cult called Aum Shinrikyo had killed twelve people and seriously injured many more by releasing deadly sarin gas into packed subway cars. When the media found out that the cult had been connected with a computer parts store and made reference to anime in its manifestos, they quickly conflated Aum with otaku as well.

American society looked down on geek culture at that time as well, but at least our geeks were portrayed as harmless nebbishes. The sensationalist media conflation of these incidents with "otaku" made it seem like Akihabara was full of killers. Okada and the Gainax animation studio had long dreamed of improving the image of "otaku." One of its more popular works was a semi-autobiographical anime called *Otaku no Video* that unabashedly embraced the pleasures of obsessive fandom. Later, Okada would write books like *Introduction to Otakuology*. Pointing out how American fans had enthusiastically embraced the term, and Japan's subcultures in general, was another angle through which

Okada could attempt to bring some respectability to the term as a vector of cultural exchange.

Okada returned from one of his American trips with his luggage loaded down with American *Star Wars* action figures—toys prized by Japanese fans, but mostly unreleased and difficult to find there.

•

Final Fantasy V has a beautiful, precise sense of pacing. At the end of the first world, you get a taste of what it's like to be all-powerful, your party full of seasoned adventurers, in command of an airship that gives you the run of the world. But once you travel to the second world, you wake up not reunited with Galuf but stranded on a tiny island, without even a chocobo to your name.

Soon after, Lenna and Faris are snatched from your camp by an enemy named Abductor, and you have to defeat the enemy using only Butz, a solo fight just like the one that began the game. The party's reunion is short-lived because they're quickly captured by the revived Exdeath and jailed in his castle. To the rescue comes Galuf, with whom the player has to single-handedly fight an Exdeath flunky named Gilgamesh to bust the rest of the party out of prison.

By adding and subtracting characters from the party, *Final Fantasy V* varies the texture of its gameplay. You may understand its systems well when you have multiple characters, but can you beat a few bosses using only one? How well-rounded are they? Which job should you choose? More than that, the game takes this moment to introduce a certain tension: When will my party come back together? When will I be able to move about freely again?

The tension and release of losing and regaining "permanent" party members and abilities can be a thrilling and rewarding experience for a player when it's crafted right, and we can see this technique used today in many other games in many other genres. In the 2012 stealth action game *Dishonored*, the main character temporarily loses all of his weapons and other gear late in the game, and has to rely only on his innate abilities until he can get them back. In Square's 2002 RPG *Kingdom Hearts*, main character Sora loses his magic Keyblade late in the game, having it replaced temporarily with a near-useless wooden sword.

Final Fantasy V is an early example of this break away from a purely linear progression in which the player simply grows more and more powerful. The more you look at it, the more you see that while its plot may be simple in its beats, the arrangement and pacing of them are master-class.

Stepping outside of Exdeath's castle and onto a massive continent-spanning bridge, the reunited party is about to face another decisive battle. It's one of the game's more memorable scenes, thanks mostly to the piece of music that accompanies it.

•

If there's any one name most closely associated with *Final Fantasy* after Hironobu Sakaguchi, it's Nobuo Uematsu, who composed the series's beautiful soundtracks. Recruited by Square in 1985, just after its founding, the self-taught Uematsu quickly became the company's favored in-house composer beginning with the 1986 Sakaguchi-designed robot mecha action game *Cruise Chaser Blassty*. Uematsu could crank out melodies as fast as Square could produce games, which was very fast: As 1987 was drawing to a close and *Final Fantasy*'s release date was drawing near, Uematsu already had a dozen soundtracks to his name.

For *Final Fantasy*, Sakaguchi gave Uematsu one direction, the same one he was following himself: Make an RPG that feels like the opposite of *Dragon Quest*. This wasn't a difficult contrast to draw since *Dragon Quest* composer Koichi Sugiyama scored the game in a distinctly Baroque classical style. (Compare the *Dragon Quest* title screen music to Vivaldi's "Spring," for example.) Uematsu's strongest musical influence at the time was 1970s piano rock. *Final Fantasy* would be Dungeons & Dragons by way of Elton John.

Much like Sakaguchi's, Uematsu's life became pretty much all Final Fantasy all the time after the success of the initial game, and he kept taking on new musical influences and crafting game after game full of memorable melodies, using the limited sound capabilities of the Famicom hardware to their fullest. (To this day I can't play *Final Fantasy II*, which has always seemed to me to be a total mess of a game, but I love the music on its own.) Uematsu's music spawned soundtrack albums (common today but still a rarity in the 80s), orchestral concerts, and millions of fans. But when it came time to compose *Final Fantasy V*, he was feeling more pressure to perform than usual.

Shortly after Nintendo released the Super Famicom in 1990, Enix, the publisher of Dragon Quest, released a game titled *Actraiser*, featuring a score from a young composer named Yuzo Koshiro. The Super Famicom's sound chip, which was designed at Sony by the eventual "father of the PlayStation" Ken Kutaragi, was incredibly capable and powerful, but operated so differently from the Famicom that game designers faced a steep learning curve. When Uematsu heard the soundtrack to *Actraiser*, he felt that it made the technical quality of his in-progress soundtrack for *Final Fantasy IV* sound weak by comparison. They hurriedly attempted to raise the quality of the sound samples for the final release, but Uematsu was still unhappy with the final product, and felt Enix had shown Square up.

Final Fantasy V was a chance to start fresh. After the up-tempo horns of its title theme music, things take a turn for the dark after the player hits Start and jumps into a new game. The music over the opening scene with Lenna, the dragon, and her father is the most complex and cinematic piece of scoring that had yet been heard in a Final Fantasy game. Rather than the usual looping melody, it's a piece that's only heard once through, its changes and inflections timed exactly to the events occurring on the screen.

When the scene fades out and comes up on Faris's pirate ship, we hear the few opening notes of the game's title theme, this time in a far more ominous key, slowly sprinkled throughout the score. There are also samples that sound like human voices, as if a choir is singing along to the music. *Final Fantasy IV* sounded like a souped-up Famicom game, but *Final Fantasy V*'s opening shows us the music team spreading its wings both technologically and creatively.

You can also spot the influence of Irish traditional music on *Final Fantasy V*. After the completion of *Final Fantasy IV*, Uematsu traveled to Dublin to record an album of Celtic-style arrangements of the game's music with a group of well-known Irish traditional musicians. "Ever since then, I've been getting deeper and deeper into Irish trad," he said in a 1997 interview. "It's the only thing I buy now, and the only thing I listen to."

The "melancholy" nature of the music, he noted, shared some similarities with the progressive rock that had also influenced the earlier Final Fantasy soundtracks. With fiddles and tin whistles fresh on his mind upon returning from Dublin, he composed a track for *Final Fantasy V* called "Harvest" that plays in some towns in the game, a lively, upbeat melody that is structured exactly like a traditional Irish jig.

But the most lasting musical impression left by *Final Fantasy V* has got to be "Battle at the Big Bridge." A rollicking, epic battle tune, it debuts as the player makes a mad dash across the bridge and away from Exdeath, fending off waves of enemies in an attempt to escape. It's often misidentified as "Battle with Gilgamesh," because that particular enemy shows up once again as you attempt to get off the bridge. Gilgamesh styles himself as a mighty warrior, but is clearly too big for his britches. "I've been waiting for you behind this door the entire time!" he says, popping out from behind a door. "I was starting to worry about what I'd do if you didn't show up."

Despite his inadequacies as a rival, he continues to show up again and again throughout the adventure as comic relief, each time believing that he has figured out the strategy that will finally take you down. Most famously, at one point he believes that he has located the legendary sword Excalibur, but it turns out that it's actually called "Excalipur" and only does 1 hit point of damage per strike.

Each time Gilgamesh shows up again (here and in cameos in future Final Fantasy games), so does that rockin' tune. Today it's considered one of the signature Final Fantasy songs in Japan. When Uematsu and some of his coworkers formed a prog-rock Final Fantasy live cover band called The Black Mages in 2003, it became one of their most-loved arrangements during live concerts. But like the rest of *Final Fantasy V*, it would take a while before it found favor with American fans.

•

I got the opportunity to begin studying the Japanese language in high school, which was a lucky break considering how unlikely it was that "potion" and "tent" comprised the entirety of the Japanese vocabulary. North Branford was just outside of New Haven, and Yale University ran an after-school program for local high schoolers who were interested in languages beyond the perfunctory French and Spanish.

In the meantime, putting together a FAQ peppered with Japanese terms might not have been the best idea when I didn't know the first thing about the language. But I had a clear vision of what I wanted to do: If Square wasn't going to release *Final Fantasy V* here, we were going to make it as accessible as possible to the English-speaking world.

The first and most basic requirement was that we were going to need to display both Japanese and English characters next to each other. Even if the reader didn't know Japanese, they could use the FAQ as a sort of Rosetta Stone, matching up the symbols they saw on the screen to the ones in the document to figure out which item they were using, which job they'd assigned their character.

Problem: Japanese language support was not a standard feature of American word processors or web browsers in 1995. Fortunately, there was a freeware word processor called NJSTAR that could handle it. Unfortunately, NJSTAR could only work with files up to a certain size, which meant we ended up having to split the FAQ into three parts. And NJSTAR was distributed over four different .ZIP files. So we were asking a lot of would-be readers on dial-up modems.

It was Nora Stevens, sitting in the computer lab at the University of Michigan, who took on the most laborious work, transcribing the Japanese characters of every single job, ability, magic spell, item, and miscellaneous piece of data in the game—then painstakingly translating them into English.

Tatsushi Nakao was writing a prose walkthrough of the game, not a step-by-step walkthrough of each floor of each dungeon, but mostly a series of notes about where to go next, who to talk to, and any particularly difficult situations a player might encounter. He was writing ahead of where I was in the game, so whenever I got to a new place, I had more of Tat's walkthrough to consult.

As for me, I was the only one currently doing a playthrough of the game as we wrote the FAQ, so I was acting as the real-time quality assurance department. Tat was writing the walkthrough from memory and using whatever Japanese materials he had around as a reference, so I was double-checking, adding extra information, and collating everything into the FAQ as the work got done.

Once we were done and ready to upload our work to the internet, we also had to make sure that the users understood that they *needed* the special word processor to read the FAQ, or the Japanese characters would just render out as gibberish ASCII code. But for all our efforts, the most common email reply that I received was, "Hey, your FAQ is all full of messed-up symbols."

Oh well. We'd tried something new, my internet friends and I, and we understood that its audience was limited by nature: How many players were going to jump through the hoops of paying exorbitant money for an old game they couldn't even read? You had to be a pretty diehard Final Fantasy fan to try that, and in 1995 there weren't that many of us.

As it turned out, though, the potential audience for *Final Fantasy V*, and our FAQ's potential reader base, was about to explode for reasons none of us had seen coming.

•

ABP, the currency that allows you to beef up your characters' job levels and thus unlock new abilities, comes slowly in *Final Fantasy V*. Most battles against standard groups of enemies give you a single, measly ABP. Many jobs require hundreds of ABP to get them to their final "master" status, at which level every ability is unlocked. And since you've probably been switching characters from job to job during the course of the game, your hard-won ABP is likely scattered amongst many different jobs at this point.

Final Fantasy V, like its immediate predecessor, is not a very grindy game: You don't have to spend hours churning through turn-based battles with random enemy mobs just to get enough strength to move on with the story. But it's certainly possible that you could make it to the end of the game with a party not so well equipped to take on the final boss battle. Perhaps anticipating this, *Final Fantasy V* has a randomly-spawning enemy that only appears near the game's final save point, called Mover. Defeat it, and you gain a whopping 199 ABP, enough to let you quickly reconfigure your party's job mix.

But that's right at the game's finale, which doesn't give you much time to really enjoy all the fancy new abilities you unlock. You might decide to try to find a good place to grind out some ABP earlier in the game so you can start playing with higher-level abilities earlier. In a cave outside the town of Jacole early in the first world, you might be battling random mobs of weak squirrels called Nuts Eaters, only to be surprised instead by a silver squirrel called Skull Eater. Maybe this superpowered cranium-devouring rodent kills your whole party. Or maybe he runs away, giving you 5 ABP, the equivalent of five ordinary battles. In my first playthrough of *Final Fantasy V*, I went on a somewhat protracted Skull Eater hunt. But ultimately, they appear too infrequently (and deal out death too easily) for this to be a viable ABP grinding spot.

There is a spot, however, early in the second world, that will let you generate insane amounts of ABP (and cash, too), enough to let you totally break the game if you want to. And I do want to. Don't you? Come on, let's break *Final Fantasy V* together.

•

We lay the groundwork for this cheeseball tactic about halfway through the first world, in the Library of the Ancients. There's a cutesy twist to the enemy battles in this dungeon: Since you're fighting books possessed by demons, each battle is presented as flipping through "pages" of the books, and fighting enemies in one-by-one succession rather than in groups.

The guy we're looking for is "Page 64," a bright blue, shiny bald, two-horned demon's head. He uses a Blue Magic spell (these, remember, can be learned if you have a Blue Mage in your party) called "Level 5 Death." If anyone in your party has a level that is any multiple of 5, they die. With a 100 percent success rate. Now, if you can learn the spell—which, yes, requires that the Blue Mage get hit by it and die in battle—you can turn this around on any enemy, even nasty bosses, with levels that are multiples of 5. (To figure out an enemy's level, you can use the spell Libra, which also lists its remaining hit points and elemental affinities. Or just use a strategy guide.)

Level 5 Death comes in handy a few times between the Library and World 2, but you can totally cash in (figuratively and literally) on it once you reach Bal Castle, the home of the no-longer-amnesiac King Galuf. The castle is mostly peaceful, a place to talk to friendly NPCs, advance the plot, buy new weapons and armor, and rest up before heading out to another dungeon. But if you head down to the castle's otherwise boring basement, an enemy called Sekizō, which simply translates to "stone statue," shows up. It's a half-broken chunk of a marble statue of a warrior in armor, come to life and very angry with you. These are liable to kill your whole party in a couple of turns, since they can and will turn you to stone. They have extremely high HP. They are best not messed with.

Or are they? A denizen of the castle gives you a helpful tip: If you take a single-use item called Gold Hairpin, which is used to turn a petrified character back to normal, and use it on the Sekizō, they'll die instantly. This turns the odds around in the battle, although it'll run you 150 gil per Hairpin. But after you win, you realize that these guys give you 4 ABP when you defeat a group of two of them, and an insane 8 ABP when you beat a group of five. You also get 507 gil per statue, enough to fund more Gold Hairpins with a lot left over.

The real secret, though, is that these guys have a level of 45. So if you learned Level 5 Death, you can instantly wipe out the whole group the second you go into battle using a single magic spell, instead of having to poke them all to death with needles one by one. Spend an hour grinding these things, and your job levels and abilities will grow so fast your head will spin. You might be tempted to spend another few hours. It's so easy to kill these things that you can zone out and forget you're playing it, which is easier when you're also watching television. I'm not ashamed to admit that the last time I played *Final Fantasy V* (on the portable PlayStation Vita) I logged about ten hours in the tiny Bal castle basement. With 90 percent of my attention devoted to watching movies, the other ten percent was creating a bunch of superpowered maniacs who could slice through most enemies in a single hit.

•

You'd be forgiven for thinking, in sending hundreds of reanimated stone statues back to hell, that you were really, truly "breaking" *Final Fantasy V*. That you'd found some sort of exploit or loophole. But every piece of this puzzle was deliberately put there for you to find. The game's designers deliberately set the Sekizō's level to 45, and they understood the implications. The vast amounts of cash and ABP held by these monsters? Also deliberate. The statues also dole out unusually *low* amounts of experience points, another deliberate decision that makes it so grinding them would barely affect your characters' base stats. In other words, you could make your characters more powerful through grinding Sekizō, but only if you had a good plan for what jobs and abilities they'd be learning. You couldn't just use them to build up brute strength.

Hironobu Sakaguchi and his team knew precisely what they'd built. (Nobuo Uematsu even mentioned this specific grinding spot in a 1993 interview.) In fact, Sakaguchi tells me, they understood their game from top to bottom, and this was all a consequence of how he had structured the development team within the greater Square organization.

Not everyone on the team was working at the same time. "The programmers and the designers were pretty much on there from beginning to end," Sakaguchi says. But, for example, the graphic artists did most of their work during the first half of the development cycle, and didn't have much to do after that.

"There wasn't a lot of last-minute iteration" on the game's graphics, he said. What would typically happen at that point is that the game's artists would mostly be moved on to other projects within Square that were at an earlier point in the development cycle.

"But I refused to let that happen with the Final Fantasy team," Sakaguchi said. Sakaguchi was Square's golden boy and Final Fantasy its flagship series, and he could ask for special treatment. Not only did he have his pick of the company's top talent, he also wanted them to create Final Fantasy and only Final Fantasy.

"I wanted everyone who was on the team from the start to be there until everything was finished," Sakaguchi said. "I wanted that commitment level." So once the graphic designers were done drawing the fantastic beasts and worlds of the game, they playtested the game, finding and documenting bugs for the programmers to fix.

Although character designer Tetsuya Nomura's first proper Final Fantasy game was *FF5*, he joined the company just before development began, and so was asked to help debug *Final Fantasy IV* before he drew a single monster. "Back then, anyone who worked on the graphics side, that was by default," Sakaguchi said. The graphic designers would finish their work early then move over to debugging until it was time to start concepting the next game in the series. "That came with the job."

Square did not yet have a "legitimate" quality assurance department, Sakaguchi said, which is why the task of bug-fixing fell to the design team. But this meant that by the time development was over, everyone was intimately familiar with the ins and outs of the game's elaborate design.

The music team's work went a little later into the cycle, but once the songs were composed, they too would sit down and help debug. "Yes," Sakaguchi says, "that does mean that Uematsu-san did debugging, too."

With the game finalized, the Final Fantasy team would go home for a month-long vacation, returning 30 days later to start on the next game. While they were on break, the finished game would finally be released to the public.

•

The release of *Final Fantasy V* on December 6, 1992 was noted in that day's *Yomiuri* newspaper, in a column titled "Graphics are Final Fantasy's Strategy."

"They say, of the two professional baseball leagues: 'The Central League may be more popular, but the Pacific League is stronger,'" the column began. "If we apply this to the world of role-playing games, perhaps we might say: '*Dora-kue* is more popular, but FF is stronger.'"

Dora-kue is an abbreviation for *Doragon Kuesuto*, which is how the phrase "Dragon Quest" would be rendered in the Japanese syllabary. The Japanese love borrowing foreign words, but the process of transliteration means that short phrases like "Dragon Quest" become, in this case, eight-syllable monstrosities that can be difficult to utter repeatedly in casual conversation. So phrases borrowed from English would often be abbreviated in this way for convenience, taking the first one or two syllables of each word. *Sutābakkusu* (Starbucks) becomes *sutaba*. *Buraddo Pitto* (Brad Pitt) becomes *Burapi*.

But this didn't need to be spelled out for the readers, as the next line of the story reads: "'*Dora-kue*' is the incredibly popular Dragon Quest, well-known to even those who don't play video games. But what is 'FF'?"

FF, the writer explained, was Final Fantasy, a game series that he suggested might actually be superior to Japan's beloved Dragon Quest: While both games featured excellent RPG design, he noted that the "high-tech" Final Fantasy had graphics that looked much better than Dragon Quest's. "That's the only way I can think of to contrast them."

While sales of Final Fantasy games had increased steadily since the first installment, prior to the release of *Final Fantasy V*, the series was still lagging behind Dragon Quest. Sales were flat: *Final Fantasy IV* had only sold a few thousand more copies than *Final Fantasy III*, while 1990's *Dragon Quest IV* again shattered the three million unit mark.

It's not clear what happened that changed Final Fantasy's fate. Perhaps word-of-mouth had reached fever pitch. Perhaps the idea that "Dragon Quest is more popular, but Final Fantasy is stronger" had reached critical mass. Maybe the fact that the Final Fantasy team had moved to the Super Famicom before the Dragon Quest team did gave them an advantage.

Whatever happened, Final Fantasy sales took off like a rocket beginning with *FF5*. It even made international headlines. "Earlier this month, the entire stock of one software game—900,000 copies—was sold on the first day it appeared in the shops," reported the *Financial Times* of London. *Final Fantasy V*, the paper summarized semi-accurately, "is set in medieval times with four knights trying to conquer a monster."

All told, *Final Fantasy V* sold about 2.4 million copies, shattering the series's previous numbers and coming achingly close to outselling *Dragon Quest V*, which had been released just a few months prior. At 2.8 million units, it was still the number one game series in town, but Final Fantasy had finally established itself as a force to be reckoned with.

To look at the sales history of the series is to be confronted, again, with the strange facts of *Final Fantasy V*'s international reputation: The "weird black sheep" of the series was, in fact, the series's first explosive mainstream hit.

•

The summer of '96. After a six-year run as the reigning champ of video game consoles, the Super Famicom/ Super Nintendo was about to be replaced by the Nintendo 64. (This time, Nintendo picked one name for the whole world.) I'd pre-ordered mine for launch day, but got to try out the machine a little early at a demonstration kiosk in our local Toys 'R' Us. I rushed home and wrote up a piece for that summer's issue of *Video Zone*, blown away by the 3D graphics and analog control of *Super Mario 64*. I was confident that this was a major turning point in the evolution of video games.

On the adjacent page, I wrote about something else I'd played for the first time over that summer break. I didn't understand it at the time, but I'd actually been playing something that would have a far greater impact on the medium of games than even *Mario 64*. It was ColEm, a piece of software for the PC that could play games that originally appeared on a 1983 game system called the ColecoVision. I didn't really spend that much time messing around with ColEm, as ColecoVision was a bit before my time, but as a proof of concept it was intriguing. I didn't have to hook up a ColecoVision and collect all of its cartridges to experience these games. I could just download them to my PC and run them whenever I wanted to.

And there were other such "emulators," I quickly discovered as I used that new search term to poke around the fast-growing internet, that could turn my PC into other old gaming machines. In fact, by the end of 1996, ColEm's author Marat Fayzullin had released iNES, which wasn't the first piece of software to attempt to emulate the Nintendo Entertainment System or Famicom, but was certainly the first user-friendly one.

The NES was a more difficult system to emulate, not least because most games developed after *Super Mario Bros.* in 1985 had extra hardware added on to their cartridge boards to soup up their power. So in 1996, while emulation of the NES was technically possible, there were few games that were compatible with the emulators, and even these didn't didn't run perfectly.

What nobody expected was just how quickly the emulators would improve. NES emulators advanced rapidly in terms of accuracy and compatibility, and hackers raced to "dump" the data from all the NES and Famicom cartridges they could get their hands on, so that they could be shared online. Within months, emulators for more powerful hardware like the Super Famicom started appearing as well. These were initially even less functional since the Super hardware was a much more complex beast, but passionate hobbyist programmers (who, like we FAQ writers, used the internet to share information and collaborate) plugged away at it so furiously that by the end of the 1990s, with Super Nintendo still on store shelves around the world, you could play most of its games on your PC with only a few bugs and glitches.

This meant that the audience for *Final Fantasy V* exploded. No longer did you have to buy a Super Nintendo, rip out the tabs, and import the cartridge. Whoever you were, wherever you lived, *Final Fantasy V* was a few mouse-clicks away. And if you wanted to navigate it, you were going to need our FAQ.

I soon started receiving a new kind of email: Players were dismayed that our walkthrough of the game did not include instructions on how to solve the "water maze puzzle." We did not include said solution, I hasten to inform you, because *Final Fantasy V* does not have a water maze puzzle.

I quickly ascertained what was happening: One of the Super Famicom's more impressive and unique hardware features, with which emulators struggled for years, was transparency. In the Grave of Ships very early in the adventure, the characters walk through pirate ships that are completely submerged in water, which is a semi-transparent blue graphical layer that sits on top of the background graphics. But the emulators of that time could only render that layer as solid blue, making it impossible to find one's way through the dungeon.

Eventually, players figured the "maze" out through trial and error—or, if the emulator supported it, by turning off the display of the individual graphic layers.

They wanted to play *Final Fantasy V*, and a little thing like not being able to see wasn't going to stop them.

While game publishers were none too thrilled that their copyrighted content was being distributed for free all over the world, there was nothing they could do about it. Games, thanks to their minuscule file sizes, were merely the vanguard. Soon, it would be music. Movies. Anime. Manga. For corporations, it was about the emerging problem of piracy. But for you and me, the internet was bringing an end to the age of scarcity.

•

The summer of 1995 brought with it another watershed event in the making of many American otaku: the American premiere of *Sailor Moon* on network television. While other anime had been shown on TV before and certainly were available on VHS tape for exorbitant prices, the fact that a contemporary 1990s show was being broadcast for free on a daily basis was a huge deal. Even if you weren't that into magical girl anime, beggars couldn't be choosers, right?

I personally was *totally* into magical girl anime, which caused my mom no end of consternation when her fifteen-year-old son, who once had to be forcibly roused out of bed to get to school on time, was now waking up at 6:30 a.m. on the dot to get a tape into the

VCR to record the ongoing saga of a group of giggling teenage girls and their cat. But I think I would have watched it even if I wasn't into the subject matter, as it was one more portal into that elusive other world.

Emboldened by my success in importing and taming *Final Fantasy V*, and with at least a little Japanese language under my belt, I started looking around to see what else was out there that I might want to attempt to import. I'd read on the internet about the existence of a Final Fantasy anime, even seen miniature blurry screen captures. A trip to a comic book store in 1996 that sold bootleg stuff taught me about "fansubs," anime subtitled into English by enthusiasts using consumer-level video editing software, and distributed from peer to peer.

Today, you can watch almost any anime that isn't distributed officially in your country thanks to fansubs, and it's usually as easy as downloading or streaming them in HD. Back then, distribution was a decidedly more analog solution. You found somebody nice who would copy the tapes for you. Arriving home from that comic store, I searched online and found a web site, probably on GeoCities, that told me if I mailed some blank VHS tapes and a token fee to the site's operator, he would copy the complete *Final Fantasy* anime onto said tapes and mail them back.

Or he'd just take the money and run, of course. And yet somehow, he did not, and I soon found myself the owner of two copied tapes containing the entirety of *Final Fantasy*, the animated miniseries. Which, I soon found out, was actually based on *Final Fantasy V*.

●

Released in 1994 in Japan across four 30-minute VHS tapes, *Final Fantasy* had some big-name talent behind it. Its director, who went by the pseudonym Rintaro, was a former disciple of "god of manga" Osamu Tezuka. Rintaro had directed episodes of the original *Astro Boy* and the film *Galaxy Express 999,* and would go on to direct 2001's *Metropolis*.

Sadly, *Final Fantasy* didn't turn out as good as any of those projects. Or any good at all, really. Set two hundred years after *Final Fantasy V*, its main character is Linaly, a teenage girl descended from Butz who has to protect the Wind Crystal from another one-dimensional big bad. The only returning character from the game is a little boy named Mid. Who's Mid? Well, every Final Fantasy game has a character named Cid who builds airships. *FF5*'s version of Cid has a young grandson who assists him. That's Mid.

The anime's plot has a pretty damn gruesome continuation of Cid and Mid's story, which we see in a flashback about midway through. After *Final Fantasy V*'s conclusion, Cid dies of old age, but after he's buried, an evil creature shows up, cuts open his skull with a massive sword and steals his genius brain, shown oozing and dripping in the monster's claws. When little Mid objects to this act of corpse defilement, the creature shoots laser eye beams through his body, killing him instantly. That's how Mid shows up 200 years later as the only returning character: as a helpful (if mischievous) ghost.

But don't worry, fans: Even though Butz doesn't appear in the anime, a lot of butts do. Mostly Linaly's. At first it's the sort of thing you see in many anime, with the main character's short skirt constantly getting blown upwards, exposing her panties. Maybe a little gratuitous to American audiences but not out of the ordinary for anime.

But early in the adventure, the Wind Crystal, for what are surely Important Reasons, hides itself inside Linaly's butt and stays there for the duration of the series. And once or twice an episode, her butt starts glowing and every character within earshot gathers around to stare good and close at her underpants. This all culminates at the end of the series when she finally farts a massive Wind Crystal-powered energy beam out of her ass.

Hey, I don't consider myself above the occasional moment of juvenile or risqué humor in my anime. (And it's not like the Final Fantasy games were *completely* G-rated: Sakaguchi and team put a stripper into *Final*

Fantasy IV, a game that also has a well-hidden "porno mag" item that, when used, causes the screen to turn pink temporarily.) But to write the entire plot of a Final Fantasy-based anime around a paper-thin excuse to stare at a girl's butt was a sad misuse of a great franchise. It didn't seem like it was done with any respect for or understanding of what made the source material appealing in the first place.

Ironically, after I jumped through so many hoops to watch the *Final Fantasy* anime, it was officially released in the US on VHS in 1997 as *Final Fantasy: Legend of the Crystals*. *Final Fantasy V*, the game it was based on, wasn't even available here yet.

Officially, anyway.

•

With few exceptions, the places you encounter in early Final Fantasy games are not by themselves spectacular. The games tend to be assemblages of standard medieval fantasy locales: forests, caves, castles. The same graphical tiles had to be repurposed multiple times within a game to create many different locations, so they had to be fairly generic in form.

What brought Final Fantasy worlds to life were by and large the monsters. Random battle encounters were the meat of the gameplay, and since enemies were invisible until the battle began, each encounter was its own surprise, not just in which monsters you stumbled across but how many of them and in what combination.

It's no secret that the original *Final Fantasy* was populated straight out of the Dungeons & Dragons *Monster Manual*. Yes, many of the D&D monsters were themselves pulled from folk tales and ancient myths, but most of them were changed quite a bit for the pen-and-paper RPG, and *Final Fantasy* copied these traits to the letter. (The sixth creature in the *Monster Manual* is a giant flightless bird with a massive beak.) The most notorious example was Beholder, a floating eyeball with smaller eyeballs growing off its flesh in gruesome stalks—this was a D&D original that *Final Fantasy* copied exactly. Square changed its name and appearance for every subsequent version of the game, presumably to avoid legal trouble.

Final Fantasy V retained many of the D&D monsters that had now become a part of Final Fantasy tradition, but after five iterations the series was beginning to put together its own original monster aesthetic as well. *Final Fantasy V*'s bestiary is still populated with *Monster Manual* enemies, but it also has its fair share of robots and machines, which have been a staple of the series since the first game's "Warmech" enemy. This seems to imply, in each game, the previous existence of a long-gone but highly advanced civilization, Sakaguchi's nod to the sci-fi he loved as much as fantasy.

But if *Final Fantasy V* made any one major addition to the series's monster mix, it's the sudden population of enemies who are extremely... *cute*. There were those adorable Nuts Eater squirrels and their deadly Skull Eater cousins. There's Gayla Cat, a cat that can fly only because it has strapped itself to a pair of homemade wings. (This is almost surely a pun on "Gayla kite," an American kite brand successful in Japan in the 1970s.)

And though they weren't enemy creatures and had already made a brief appearance in *Final Fantasy III* years prior, *Final Fantasy V* was the first game in the series to prominently feature the Moogles (written in English as "Moglies" in Japan), a race of winged teddy-bear-like creatures with magic powers and a love of saying the word "Kupo!"

This new emphasis on cute was at least partially because of the influence of Tetsuya Nomura, the young artist who'd joined just in time to debug *Final Fantasy IV* but cut his teeth as a designer on *FF5*. Artists, even newbies like Nomura, were given a lot of leeway to design the sorts of things they wanted to, he said in a 2001 interview. Sakaguchi and Kitase would ask for "simple requests, like 'a robot' or 'a dragon,'" he said, and leave him to fill in the rest. "I'm bad at drawing robots," said Nomura. "I designed things like people and animals. Like the Goblins, or the Nuts Eater."

In a later interview, Nomura recalled that Sakaguchi and Kitase soon began to take a particular interest in his concepts. "Everyone else used computers to type things out for their main plan books, but in order to have more impact, I wrote all the notes by hand and included plenty of drawings," he said. "After a while, whenever it was time to turn in our plan books, Sakaguchi and Kitase would say 'Where's Tetsu's plan book?' as they started looking forward to it each time."

Nomura loved mixing cute and deadly, as evidenced by his most enduring *Final Fantasy V* creation, a monster called Tonberi. Asked to create a "half-man, half-fish" type character, Nomura turned in what looks like an adorable little baby lizard with a round head and a squat frame, wearing a Yoda robe, carrying a lantern in his left hand and a chef's knife in his right. He does nothing for a few seconds, then he disappears. Is the fight over? No, because soon after he reappears, slightly closer to the heroes. This is quite a surprising moment that can throw you off your game, as nearly every enemy in a *Final Fantasy* game prior to this has stood stock-still for the duration of the battle, keeping a respectful distance. But this guy? He's inching closer and closer to you.

Finally, Tonberi reaches the group of heroes, pulls out his chef's knife, and straight up kills one of you in a single shot, no matter how powerful you are. Then he returns to his original position and starts advancing again.

Tonberi, like the Moogles, has been a perennial fan favorite and is a big seller in stuffed-animal form in Japan, although I don't think I'd want one on my pillow when the lights go out.

·

Square never totally gave up on the idea of releasing *Final Fantasy V* outside Japan. In 1996, Square and Nintendo parted ways, and Square shifted all of its development to the Sony PlayStation. This put a final nail in the coffin of releasing the Super Famicom version here as *Final Fantasy Extreme*.

Square had partnered with the Western game publisher Eidos to release a Windows PC version of its PlayStation game *Final Fantasy VII*, and as a follow-up began pursuing the idea of converting *Final Fantasy V* to the PC as well. It hired an Austin, Texas developer called Top Dog Software to port the game to Windows 95, and had the text of the game translated into English for this purpose. It announced that the game was coming to PC, and even released some work-in-progress screenshots. But the project was canceled midway through.

This would have been more disappointing were it not for the fact that if you owned a Windows PC in 1997, you could already play an English-language version of *Final Fantasy V*.

•

The first "ROM hack" I ever remember playing was called *Nude Punch-Out*. A hacker by the handle of (I swear this is true) ExDeath edited the graphics data of the popular NES game *Mike Tyson's Punch-Out!!*, erased all the opposing boxers' shorts, and drew dicks on them. Bald Bull and Mr. Sandman, who shared sprite data from the neck down, each got a vulva instead. *Nude Punch-Out* was crude, of no redeeming value, and a big hit at college parties.

Modifying computer programs to change their functionality had long been an intrinsic, even expected, aspect of personal computing. Now that NES games had been liberated from their frozen sleep on the static layers of ROM chips and repurposed into copyable, editable file formats, of course players would start playing around with the code itself. And it wasn't long before some started wondering, could the same tools used to draw a boner on Piston Honda be used to insert English text into Japanese RPGs?

It wasn't as easy as all that, and in fact required a great deal of specialized programming knowledge. But as with the development of emulators, "fan translations" evolved from crazy idea to established reality with what now seems like astonishing rapidity. Although a few different loosely-connected online groups attempted to translate the *Final Fantasy V* file into English beginning in 1996, it was a group called RPGe that got the job done over a period of four months in the summer of 1997. They'd translated everything except for some scrolling text at the game's finale, which must have proven too tricky a bit of programming to crack. By mid-1998 they'd figured that out, too. The engineer behind the project, who reprogrammed the Super Famicom game to display English using amateur tools, was a high school student from California.

In translating the game into English, the unofficial group made at least one localization choice that endures to this day. When Nora, Tat, and I were putting together our FAQ, we were scraping together whatever information we could and making educated guesses to fill in the gaps about what things should be called in English. For the name of Galuf's granddaughter, Krile, we just wrote down the Roman alphabet equivalent of the Japanese characters that displayed for her name.

Sakaguchi loved giving his characters elaborate Western European names, but it can be difficult to render some of these into the rigid Japanese syllabary, which (simply speaking) requires that consonants and vowels be evenly dispersed throughout the words. My first name, for instance, would have to be written with the *katakana* characters クリス, pronounced "ku-ri-su." Krile (pronounced something like *cur*-ul) was written as クルル, "ku-ru-ru," which we wrote in the FAQ as Kururu.

The name did not exactly trip lightly off the tongue. Koo*roo*roo? Koo*koo*roo? Kookaburra? Well, like it or not, that was definitely what the game said—and that's all we had to go on. Although English versions of many characters' names written in the Roman alphabet appeared somewhere in the three volumes that made up the official *Final Fantasy V* guide, "Krile" was not one of them. It's likely that the name "Krile" appeared in some supplemental Japanese materials that none of us owned, but all we knew was "Kururu."

The vast majority of the transliteration choices the RPGe crew made lined up with the official English spellings of the words that were found in the Japanese strategy guides. They only made a few major deviations, using "Worus Castle" instead of "Walse Castle," for example. But there was one nut they just couldn't crack. "Kururu's name was an enigma to us," says "Myria," the engineer on the team. They, too, had searched all of the resources they could, but came up empty. "We didn't really know what to call her."

"SoM2Freak," one of the two translators on the project, suggested renaming her "Cara," changing a difficult-to-pronounce, rough-sounding name to something softer and more familiar to American ears. It was a decision that a professional localization team might have made, for the same reasons that Square's Ted Woolsey changed some names around in *Final Fantasy VI*. Myria says she disagreed with SoM2Freak's decision. "I personally didn't think that it matched Kururu, but I didn't fight him much over it," she said. So "Cara" it was.

"Cara" has had tremendous staying power: As of 2017, a Google search for "final fantasy v cara" returns twice as many results as "final fantasy v krile." And why shouldn't it? For many players, the fan translation is the only *Final Fantasy V* they know.

Fan translation of console games began with *Final Fantasy V*, but it didn't end with it. By the end of 2016, the website ROMhacking.net had listed 925 games translated into English by fans that are marked as "fully playable," that is, translated from start to finish. Many more RPGs besides *Final Fantasy V* didn't get an official English release back in the day, but fans have now accomplished what the game publishers of the time couldn't or wouldn't.

•

Hironobu Sakaguchi's reputation in the Japanese video game scene of the 1990s was like George R.R. Martin's in the literary world today: It seemed like the creator of Final Fantasy delighted in creating fan-favorite characters only to kill them off with extreme prejudice.

Many of the new Final Fantasy fans who got into the series with the seventh installment on the PlayStation were crushed beyond repair to witness the death of innocent flower girl Aeris. But longtime fans were used to seeing our favorites wiped out, whether non-playable side characters or actual party members.

In *Final Fantasy IV*, the sage Tellah went from party MVP to roadkill in nothing flat, while other extremely useful party members (four of them, actually: Yang, Cid, Palom, and Porom) also had a habit of sacrificing their lives to save the rest of the party. Even if they were revealed to be alive and well later, the pain at that moment of losing the characters was multiplied. Not only did you not want their story arc to end in tragedy, but they were so damn useful in your party. (And woe betide you if you left any good weapons or armor equipped on them when they bit the big one, because those were gone forever.)

With *Final Fantasy V*, Sakaguchi had the opportunity to step it up. Your characters weren't just social butterflies who flitted in and out of the party, as with the fourth game. This was a group of characters that you'd lovingly built up piece by piece, tweaking their abilities and jobs until they were running like a fine-tuned machine. What if one of them were to die? Would you lose it? Throw your controller? Bawl like a baby?

Sakaguchi, who loved making players cry, wanted to find out. And to give the scene maximum impact, he says he looped the game's battle designers in on crafting the storyline.

Galuf's final moments take place in the Grand Forest of Moore, a pivotal location in the plot of *Final Fantasy V*. It was here, long before the events of the game, that humans had sealed away all the evil spirits of the world in a tree, which soon became so consumed by evil that it grew into a single being of pure evil, Exdeath. Exdeath confronts the party here in the Guardian Tree, using the powers of its crystals to nearly kill them. Krile attempts a daring rescue, but Exdeath quickly overpowers her as well.

It's seeing his granddaughter in peril that causes Galuf to stand up, fight through Exdeath's magic, and engage him one-on-one in battle. Exdeath quickly unleashes numerous attacks that bring Galuf's hit points down to 0, but the old man refuses to die. He pushes through with superhuman strength.

"The battle team wasn't just there to create the battles," Sakaguchi says. Since the team size was still only about fifteen people, he says, it was much easier to have cross-discipline collaboration. "The direction of that scene, down to the details, that was a collaboration of ideas coming from the battle team: What can we do to make it more dramatic, to leave that headstrong impression of what he said right before he was killed off?"

"Wh... why won't you die?" Exdeath screams.

"Not yet!" Galuf replies. "I ain't dying yet!" The two continue to trade barbs, culminating in Galuf fending off, but not killing, Exdeath. But his wounds are too great, and after some parting words to his now-safe group, Galuf dies. A few nail-biting minutes later, the player finds out that at least all his or her effort has not been for nothing, as Galuf passes his abilities and experience onto Krile, who joins the party for the game's third and final act.

The death of Galuf, far from an arbitrary choice, is actually quite important to the theme of the game. *Final Fantasy V* is about parents and children, a meditation on passing the mantle of responsibility to the younger generation. Galuf was one of the four adventurers who, along with Butz's dad, sealed away Exdeath in the first place. He had his adventure long ago. This isn't his story.

•

As the game's second act comes to a close, *Final Fantasy V* again shows its mastery of pacing. With Galuf's death still stinging in their minds (and the player's), the reformed party begins its presumably final assault on Exdeath's castle. And indeed, it feels much like a final dungeon. After regaining entrance to the keep in which some of your partymates were formerly imprisoned, the crew soon discovers that its standard medieval castle appearance is a facade, and Exdeath's keep is actually a gruesome living tower of flesh. It's packed with massive, brutal monster encounters, a miniboss, and finally Exdeath himself, standing almost the entire height of the television screen in his suit of armor, packing tons of hit points and debilitating attacks.

Now, if you're familiar with other Final Fantasy games, you realize that this boss battle is not exactly *epic* enough, not exactly *I just killed God himself* enough to be the final battle. The real end boss of a Final Fantasy usually looks like somebody glued together ten William Blake paintings. But hey, if you're one of the million Japanese players who bought *Final Fantasy V* in 1992 but not *Final Fantasy IV*, maybe you don't know this. And when the party wakes up in a craggy field after Exdeath's castle goes kaboom, maybe you think you won the game.

It certainly seems like the story is wrapping itself up nicely. The group finds itself back home in front of

Castle Tycoon, and the kingdom is overjoyed to see the return of their princess Lenna, and also Faris, who earlier in the game was revealed to be Lenna's long-lost sister Sarisa. (The gruff-talkin' lady pirate is made to put on a dress for the royal celebration, and we get a humorous scene of Butz going goggle-eyed at her beauty, tiny hearts appearing out of his sprite's head.)

With Lenna and Faris consumed with their royal duties, Butz and Krile decide to ride Boko around a bit. They soon find themselves trapped in a creature's den, and are rescued by Faris, who's ditched the dress and the royal life entirely to keep adventuring with her pals. Everything is great except Krile has a splinter in her finger that's annoying her. I mean, hey, if that's the extent of your problems...

That little splinter, though, turns out to be who else but Exdeath the Angriest Tree, who is still not dead. And there's something else fishy going on, too. Hironobu Sakaguchi prided himself on his puzzles, and he gives you a little bit of time to figure this one out for yourself. Maybe you notice that the geography around Castle Tycoon is a bit different. Maybe you found it strange that Ghido the sage, who lived in Galuf's world, is now shacking up right next door to the castle. Or maybe you didn't catch on until the game's dialogue spelled it out for you explicitly.

But eventually, you figure out what's happened. You open up the game's map screen and marvel. The first world and the second world fit together like an interlocking puzzle. Four separate continents are now one land mass. What were formerly two archipelagos of scattered islands are now one unbroken peninsula.

While you're marveling at Sakaguchi's crowning achievement, taking in what has to be the greatest Final Fantasy puzzle ever, one you didn't even know was a puzzle, the reality dawns on you: These are not two distinct planets that were put together. These are two halves of a world that were ripped apart, and have now been put back where they belonged. There was never "one world" and the "other world." What appeared at first to be a separate plane of existence, unreachable and untouchable, was just the other part of the world you had always lived in. Perhaps the world is smaller than it first appeared to be. But it was also far more connected than you had ever imagined.

THE MERGED WORLD

WHILE I WAS DROOLING OVER the Nintendo 64 in 1996, in the back of my mind I knew that eventually I'd also have to buy a Sony PlayStation. Fortunately I had a job ringing up groceries, and although I wasn't exactly pulling down pachinko cash like some other people I could name, I made enough that I no longer had to restrict myself to a single gaming console. It was already obvious that most of the game series I loved were abandoning Nintendo and migrating to Sony, Final Fantasy foremost among them.

The reason why was simple. The Nintendo 64 used ROM cartridges while PlayStation used compact discs. The CD-ROM medium offered vastly more storage than cartridges, and was much cheaper to manufacture. As the *Yomiuri* newspaper's technology column noted in 1992, Square had always been about cutting-edge graphics. Even back in the days of programming for Japanese personal computers, it boasted of its ability to draw more detailed, speedier graphical displays than its competitors. While Square could have made a Final Fantasy on the Nintendo 64, the PlayStation offered Square a way to create cinematic sequences rendered by high-powered computers and then include as video clips the most advanced graphic sequences ever seen in any console game. The videos would take up tons of memory, but that was not an issue with PlayStation—*Final Fantasy VII* could ship on three CD-ROM discs for almost no extra cost.

PlayStation had a lot of solid games, but it didn't yet have a *Mario 64*, a killer app, a system-seller. *Final Fantasy VII*'s graphics and movie sequences were so beautiful and so cutting-edge that they stood above practically anything else on consoles at the time, and pulled in many players who had never tried an RPG before in their lives. In Japan, it was the first game in the series to sell more than three million copies—although it was still outsold by its eternal rival *Dragon Quest VII* a few years later.

But this time, there was a big difference. While *Dragon Quest VII* only moved about 200,000 copies outside Japan, overseas sales of *Final Fantasy VII* totaled well over five million. Final Fantasy's quest to unseat Dragon Quest as the king of RPGs was over. And it achieved the victory thanks to its new fans in the West.

Having cut ties with Nintendo and established the PlayStation as the new home of Final Fantasy, Square looked forward to creating new games on the platform. But it also looked back into its past. Now that Final Fantasy was one of gaming's hottest brands worldwide, perhaps it could get some new life out of its classics?

On March 21, 1997, Square released a version of *Final Fantasy IV* for the PlayStation exclusively in Japan. The computer graphics wizards that crafted *Final Fantasy VII*'s cinematic sequences created new opening and ending scenes to bookend the Super Famicom game, turning its tiny sprite characters into realistic humans (by 1997's creepy-doll uncanny valley standards, anyway). The sound was a little off and it took forever to save your progress, but it was a second chance at a solid game for new fans ready to catch up.

A year later, Square released a PlayStation version of *Final Fantasy V* with similar upgrades. A year after that, it finished the Super Famicom trilogy with an enhanced version of *Final Fantasy VI*, and also sold the games in a three-game boxed set called *Final Fantasy Collection*.

So far, these PlayStation re-releases were only available in Japan, but Square fans outside the country saw this as a golden opportunity to finally get *Final Fantasy V* on these shores. As Sakaguchi recalls, this had always been in the cards. "They were probably ported to PlayStation because we wanted to release them overseas," he says. After the release of *Final Fantasy Collection* in 1999, Square had good news and bad news for its American fans. Yes, it would finally bring *Final Fantasy V* to the US as part of a package called *Final Fantasy Anthology*. The bad news was that this time it was *Final Fantasy IV* getting passed over for a US release, and the package would only contain *Final Fantasy V* and *VI*.

In a comment to an RPG enthusiast website called Gaming Intelligence Agency, which was Andrew Vestal's next project after the shutdown of the UnOfficial Squaresoft Home Page, Square's US branch explained the move: "The texts of *Final Fantasy V* and *Final Fantasy VI* were already translated into English. We once planned to release PC versions of these titles in English, although that plan was canceled."

So the release of *Final Fantasy V* on PlayStation was simply the latest, and final, event in the ongoing saga of the game's on-again, off-again English release. Had the PC project never been in the works, *Final Fantasy Anthology* might never have been released in any state. Square was only releasing *Final Fantasy V* and *VI* because 99 percent of the work was already done, and it said that it wanted its localization team to focus on "more recent titles" in lieu of re-translating *Final Fantasy IV*.

On September 30, 1999, *Final Fantasy V* was finally officially released in North America. We'd finally caught the one that got away. But the victory would be bittersweet.

•

While it was certainly nice to have Final Fantasy games available in English, the quality of the text translation in the American versions often left something to be desired. Nintendo's script for the first game in the series was fairly good by 1990's standards, if sometimes a little unnatural. ("I, Garland, will knock you all down!") Square's translation of *Final Fantasy IV* fared worse, with clunky writing to the point of weird: "Dwarf armors are hard! Can you move in it?" Some bits were translated incorrectly, and many of the finer details and nuances had to be sliced out of the script so the English would fit where the Japanese had been.

Japanese games translated by a non-native speaker of English tended to read strangely. But even if a talented, native writer was put on the project, they often didn't get the support or tools they needed to do a decent job. They were usually working under intense time constraints. They often weren't even able to speak to the original development team, as Jeremy Blaustein, the translator of *Dragon Quest VII*, said in a 2016 interview: "When a game's done, they put everything down and they take a vacation, and then they get on to their next project. [When they] started [working] again, the teams would be mixed up. Different people would be assigned to different projects, completely busy with them, and their bosses wouldn't want you bothering them about a previous game... no answers, no help, no organization, no idea what's going on."

Ted Woolsey's 1994 translation of *Final Fantasy VI* is some of the best localization of the era. Written naturally, even beautifully at times, it brings across the feeling of the original in a way that previous games' English scripts utterly failed to. Woolsey still had to slice and dice lots of content out of the script, and was still under extreme time pressure, but he made a serious effort to compress and retain as much as humanly possible.

Final Fantasy VII, translated with haste and sloppiness by Sony, was an unfortunate step backward. But by the time it released *Final Fantasy VIII* in 1999, translated and published in-house, Square regained its footing. Had the Square of 1999 translated *Final Fantasy V*, it would likely have been a decent piece of work. But that's not what happened. Square took the pre-existing text from the aborted PC game and dropped it into the PlayStation port as-is. And thus it came to pass that the *Anthology* version of *Final Fantasy V* received what is, beyond all doubt, the worst official translation that any Final Fantasy game has ever been saddled with.

•

If you can think of a type of translation error, the *Anthology* version of *Final Fantasy V* surely commits it many times. The first thing you'll notice (besides the leaden prose and general aversion to words longer than two syllables) is the weird formatting, with dropped punctuation and oddly-placed line breaks all over.

One of Lenna's first lines after she meets Butz has a grammatical error: "This thing just fell out of sky," she says, gazing at the meteor.

Faris is, of course, a pirate, and so it would only make sense to spice up her accent with some seafarin' jargon here and there. Instead, *Final Fantasy V*'s translation team seemed to make a game of attempting to turn *every single word* Faris says into its Talk Like a Pirate Day equivalent, resulting in sentences like "Avast! What're ye doin' thar?" Also, every sentence possible had to be punctuated with "D'aar!" or "T'aar!" (Remember: when in doubt, consonant + "aar" = instant pirate.)

This tendency towards ridiculous language when plain language is called for is most apparent in the message that appears after every successful battle (meaning about a thousand times in the course of one playthrough). The original line translates to "You won the battle!" I can think of a dozen appropriate English equivalents that would have been fine. Instead of any of those, you see the message "YESSSSSSSS!" as if Butz were a tween who just pulled off a sick kickflip.

Final Fantasy V's localization choices are also broadly inconsistent with other games in the series. The battle cry of the dwarf characters has been romanized as either "Lali-ho!" or "Rally-ho!," but here it's "Tally-ho!" because nobody checked. Even worse, *Final Fantasy V* is also inconsistent with *itself*. Example: The translators renamed the "Gold Hairpin" item that cures characters turned to stone to the more straightforward "Soft," but then forgot to alter the once-helpful line from a villager that reads "stone-like monsters can't stand Gold Hairpins."

And when you arrive at the Fork Tower, a dungeon that requires you to split your party up into physical attackers and magic users, a mistranslated pair of villager lines give you the wrong information about which half of the tower is which.

Finally, whenever the translators encountered a foreign loan word written in *katakana* characters that they couldn't figure out, their solution was to just make something up. "Zephyr" became "Zefa." An enemy with the French name "Pas de Seul" became "PaddleThru." The worst and most notorious: The classic monster "Wyvern" was translated as "Y Burn."

No, sorry, I'm underselling it. The *worst* worst thing, the *coup de grace* (or, as *Anthology* would have rendered it, the CooterGraw) was that Tonberi, Nomura's iconic fan-favorite monster, was renamed "Dinglberry." In case you didn't watch much *Beavis and Butt-Head* in the 90s, a dingleberry is slang for a tiny piece of poop that clings to your butt hair after you wipe. Don't blame me for this mental image: I didn't put it in *Final Fantasy V*, Square did.

Looking back on the *Anthology* translation today, it looks to me like a rough draft. Everything was translated hastily, but nothing was tested to see how it played out in the final game and how the various parts worked with each other. Nothing was double-checked against the original intentions of the creators. There was no final editing pass. I don't blame the actual (anonymous) people who did the work, who were probably under incredible time pressure with near-zero assistance. I blame the higher-ups at a company that wanted its games to be seen as legendary masterpieces, but didn't yet believe it was necessary to translate them as such.

•

More so than "good versus evil," Final Fantasy plots often ultimately converge on a struggle between existence versus non-existence, or of order versus chaos. (The final boss of the first game is literally named "Chaos.") Many Final Fantasy villains don't dream of building an evil empire and taking over the world, they dream of *annihilating* the world. Exdeath's stated goal is to restore what is simply known as 無 (*mu*), a Japanese character meaning "nothingness."

The *mu* (translated in *Anthology* as "the Void," a pretty good translation that's stuck around in later versions of the game) isn't just an absence of existence. It's described as an all-powerful force, the state of the universe prior to the formation of matter. The pre-Big Bang, in other words.

Sakaguchi says this recurring motif is another avenue by which he attempted to blend science fiction into the fantasy RPG framework. "I told you I hated going to school," he says. "But the one subject I could tolerate was physics. All you had to do to pass the exam was memorize some formulas." From his interest in physics came an interest in astronomy. "I wanted to know more about space, and what went on there." His obsession with otherworldly beings and the vast emptiness of the universe inspired his very sci-fi plots, with villains who harnessed the power of unexplained science. The first *Final Fantasy*'s plot revolves around a time loop that the heroes have to break. *Final Fantasy IV*'s story ends on the moon.

Well-rounded people with interests in many different areas, Sakaguchi says, are the sort of people he tried to surround himself with in the creation of Final Fantasy games. "You need to combine disciplines in order to contribute to this," he says. "You can't just have people with a background in the school of arts and expect them to write these scripts. People on our team have a school of science background, but have a very passionate interest in arts."

Artists with the "Science" ability equipped, or Scientists with "Art." One hand holding a copy of *Guin Saga*, one hand on the pachinko flipper.

•

Crappy translation aside, I was happy that *Final Fantasy V* was finally available for the average player who didn't want to deal with emulators or sketchy ROM download sites, and that it was finally an "official" part of the series in America. Sure, it was stuck playing second fiddle to *Final Fantasy VI*, which was considered the real draw of the *Anthology*. Yes, it looked primitive next to Square's crowning achievement, *Final Fantasy VIII*, which had released that same month on four CD-ROMs. But it was still here.

As the de facto maintainer of the FAQ, I decided this would be a great time to do a new version specifically for the PlayStation release. I'd play through the game, update all of the names to match the new translations, and delete all of the no-longer-necessary Japanese writing.

To accompany the release of the game, two books containing *Final Fantasy V* walkthroughs were released in America. The monthly magazine *Game Informer* published a book titled *The Final Fantasy Companion*, which contained strategies for games *FF5* through *FF8*. And the publisher BradyGames, which did Square's officially licensed guides, published a *Final Fantasy Anthology* guide with strategies for both games in the collection.

I flipped open the *Game Informer* book at a local FuncoLand game store, and was aghast at what I saw. The country's most popular gaming magazine had copied and pasted our FAQ into its pages without attribution. They'd added some extra content here and there, and rewritten some of the sentences, but it was without a doubt our work. Here's a representative sample (with original errors intact).

Our FAQ: "Solitary Island: When you arrive at the second world, use "tent". (If you don't have a supply, you can fight the enemies here to obtain tent.) While you are asleep, Abductor attacks your party. You have to fight with Butz alone."

Game Informer: "Solitary Island: When get here, use a Tent. If you don't have one, the monsters you fight here will. While you're asleep, Abductor attacks. Bartz fights alone."

The plagiarism in the BradyGames guide wasn't so easily spotted, because there were no such blatant instances of identical paragraph structures. But it was there. We'd made a goof in the section of the FAQ dealing with the Phoenix Tower, which requires players to climb up 30 different floors, each with two doors. Half the doors have monsters behind them, half do not. We messed up the left-right-left-right order that would get you through with no encounters, and both guides copied the incorrect solution.

Finally, both guides listed, at the end, a "recommended party" for taking on the game's final boss. Both recommendations listed the exact same jobs and abilities, because both were simply *my party*, which was still on my save file on my original *Final Fantasy V* cartridge that I'd described in a separate FAQ I'd written alone called "The Amazing Exdeath Strategy Guide."

It would be safe to describe my emotional state at this point as "filled with impotent rage." I was already getting a little bit of freelance work here and there writing about games, but I was a nobody, and here these big names of game publishing were stealing work from internet amateurs. But what could I do? I was nineteen. I had no concept of how much money it cost to hire a lawyer. Moreover, I had written this FAQ alongside two other people I didn't really know, so I couldn't say that it was all mine.

I wrote formal letters to each publisher explaining the situation. I got no response from either. I wasn't sure where to go from there, so I complained about the plagiarism in a blistering note appended to my new version of the FAQ... and then I dropped the subject. I had bigger fish to fry, not least the fact that my junior year of college was coming up, which meant that I was going to go live in Japan in a few months' time. But it still stung.

•

Towards the end of the development of *Final Fantasy V*, someone on the team had a big idea. Unfortunately, it was not the time to be coming up with big ideas. With only a few months left in development, it was time to test, polish, and finalize the program. But this idea was too good to let go of. What if, the team thought, the abilities of any jobs that you had mastered were then absorbed by the *suppin*, or "Bare" class that you'd started the game with? So once you'd mastered a few classes, you could switch back to Bare and have a character that had the magical power of a mage, the hand-to-hand combat strength of a Monk, et cetera? It would feel like coming full circle, finishing the game just as you'd begun it, but all of the choices you'd made throughout the adventure would then combine to create an ultra-powerful character.

"At the very end, when we were supposed to be wrapping up this game, as we were testing, we thought, okay, why don't we figure this out? Because this would be such an exciting moment," Sakaguchi says. In the end, the idea was too good, and they had to cram it in at the last minute. "Even though it was really difficult, it was worth putting in the effort, because it made that feature really stand out," he says.

So when I say that I spent hours in a castle basement fighting rocks to create a character who could smash through almost anything in the game single-handedly, this is what I mean. I could have every character master the Monk class, even if they weren't going to be hand-to-hand fighters, because they'd all get a 30 percent bump to their hit points. I could master the Thief and Elemental User (aka Geomancer) classes and be able to see hidden passages and walk through magma. But truth be told, I was aiming for a specific combination of character traits that is notorious for being one of the most powerful combos in the game: *mahōken nitōryū midareuchi*, or "Magic Sword Dual-Wield Scattered Shot."

This requires that a single character master the Archer job to unlock its final ability, "Scattered Shot," which fires four arrows at random targets that do half the normal damage of one arrow, master the Ninja job which allows a character to dual-wield weapons, and achieve at least some level of proficiency with the Enchanter so that you can imbue your weapons with elemental magic powers in battle.

What makes this all work is that Scatter Shot doesn't just apply to bows and arrows. If it's learned and then used while the character has another job, they'll attack four times with whatever weapon they have equipped, doing half damage. But if they've mastered Ninja and equipped two weapons, they'll attack eight times. And if they've enchanted those weapons with magic, one single attack is the equivalent of casting one of those spells eight times in a row.

What that means in practice is Everything Dies. Even though I was barely more than halfway through the game, I switched all my characters to Bare as I came out of Bal Castle and never switched back. I was giving up on all of the ability points that I could have amassed over the rest of the game, but I didn't need them anymore.

Mahōken nitōryū midareuchi is an example of emergent gameplay. It wasn't specifically put there by the game's designers. Players developed it themselves. But it's become so legendary among *Final Fantasy V* players that it's now considered as much a part of the game as anything that Sakaguchi put there deliberately.

·

I didn't stop importing games after *Final Fantasy V*. What first seemed to be the endgame was just the intro sequence. My next conquest was *Seiken Densetsu 3*, the sequel to *Secret of Mana* that was also never released here despite the series's popularity. And when Sega prematurely discontinued the Saturn game console in the US, of course I had to buy the *X-Men vs. Street Fighter* game that was only out in Japan.

But in general, the advent of the cheap medium of CD-ROM, a growing appreciation for JRPGs in the West, and Sony effectively branding the PlayStation as a product suited for adults meant that in general, the best games were more likely to be released here. In 2001, Square even went back to that PlayStation version of *Final Fantasy IV*, finally giving it a well-done translation (and marking the first time the original, more difficult version of the game was released in America).

Meanwhile, the American market for Japanese comics and animation exploded. Manga had moved from a tiny shelf in the comic store to a large area of the mall's mainstream bookstore. It was sold as it was in Japan, in small-format paperback books, not as American-size comics. Eventually, publishers stopped "flopping" the artwork so the pages "read" left to right; they just left them in the right-to-left orientation of Japan and asked consumers to learn to read manga books "backwards." They'd leave the Japanese sound effects alone in the artwork instead of laboriously redrawing them. It saved a lot of time and money for the publishers, and fans were happier to experience the work with fewer alterations.

Just as Toshio Okada had hoped, the surging interest in Japanese pop culture in the West helped to rehabilitate the image of "otaku" at home. The highly popular 2004 novel (and movie and TV show) *Densha Otoko*, or "Train Man," was a love story that presented a sympathetic image of otaku. Taro Aso, who served as Japan's Prime Minister in 2008 and 2009, proclaimed himself an otaku who loved reading manga. In 2014, the Japanese government, under an initiative called "Cool Japan," offered $155 million worth of grants to assist in localizing and promoting Japanese pop culture content around the world.

In January 2017, Square Enix (the company formed when the makers of Final Fantasy and Dragon Quest merged in 2003) announced that platinum-selling recording artist Ariana Grande would appear as a playable character in *Final Fantasy Brave Exvius*, a mobile game with a throwback, retro 2D style reminiscent of the Super Famicom titles. For promotional use, Square Enix distributed a digital photo of the 23-year-old singer with an autograph and a quote. Above her signature,

Grande had written だいすき ("I love you") in *hiragana* characters. The quote read thusly:

> "It is an honor for my Pixel Art character and for my music to be included in the new *Final Fantasy Brave Exvius* game, a mainstay in the Japanese pop culture, which I absolutely adore."

Otaku culture is mainstream culture. In so many ways, we are living in the merged world.

•

As the first Final Fantasy game built around the idea of changing jobs freely, *Final Fantasy III* on the Famicom is the original raw vision that *Final Fantasy V* refined and polished. Although *Final Fantasy III* was a big hit, the first in the series to sell over a million copies, Sakaguchi wasn't entirely happy with how it turned out. "We were criticized for the final dungeon being too hard to beat, and we took that to heart," he says. It was a problem common in those Wild West days of Famicom game development. The game was only playtested by those who were making it, who had too much expertise in the game to understand how difficult the average player would find it.

While Sakaguchi admits that the extreme difficulty was "partially because we knew the game inside-out," he says it was also because they loved the feeling of figuring out the perfect job and ability combinations to take down seemingly impossible boss characters. "The final battle made us really excited," he says. "We were getting exhilarated trying to defeat it, and we wanted the players to feel what we were feeling."

But after *Final Fantasy III*'s release, Sakaguchi reckoned the super-hard bosses could have the opposite effect on some players. "There are going to be some players who don't get to that point, and it will sort of ruin the game and leave a bad taste in their mouths," he says. "Let's say you get stuck in *FF5*, and you gave up. I don't know if those people would want to come back and play *FF6*."

In bringing back the job change system for *Final Fantasy V*, the team wanted to try to square this circle. How could they make the game conquerable for all levels of players, but also introduce battles that required players to fully master the ins and outs of the game's systems? Eventually, they hit upon the idea that the hardest bosses in the game wouldn't be part of the main storyline, but instead be purely optional encounters. They wouldn't block off access to any part of the game, they wouldn't shower the player with luxurious rewards. The reward for conquering them would be the knowledge that you did it.

Final Fantasy V had two such encounters, both of which were palette-swapped versions of monsters found in the main storyline. Both of them were placed in the game's final dungeon. Omega was a machine that conspicuously walked around a cliffside and could be easily avoided, and Shinryū was a dragon hidden inside a treasure chest later in the dungeon.

Both enemies could wipe even a relatively powerful party out in just a couple of turns, so you had to figure out how to defeat them fast. In the Final Fantasy world (as in life), machines are weak against lightning strikes. But casting even the strongest Thunder spells on Omega wouldn't get the job done fast enough. The most popular solution, which you might have already realized, is *mahōken nitōryū midareuchi*, which allows one character to cast Thunder on Omega eight times per turn. This is easier said than done, of course, since it requires hours of ABP farming.

Similarly, for Shinryū, one could have each character master both the Dragoon and Ninja jobs, then steal eight Dragon Lances (one per hand, two per person), then use the Dragoon's Jump command to do maximal damage. This, too, requires hours upon hours of prep. There are other ways to game the system, though.

These optional "superboss" battles that originated in *Final Fantasy V* have become a staple of the series ever since. The important thing about these battles, as Andrew Vestal notes, is that you can't just grind them out. "There's no shortcuts, there's no fakery for those battles, and that is what makes them enjoyable," he says. "It doesn't matter what level you are in *Final Fantasy V*: If you want to beat Omega, you have to squeeze every last drop of gameplay out of those systems in order to succeed."

If you defeat Shinryū, you find that the treasure chest he was shacking up in contained the game's best sword, Ragnarok, which honestly you probably don't need if you were powerful enough to get it. Otherwise, defeating each of these bosses gives you a simple reward: An item that sits in your inventory to prove that you conquered the game's most difficult challenges. "We cherish the save data on our cartridges," Sakaguchi says. "It's our treasure." The items were 1992's equivalent of an Xbox Achievement, visible proof of your greatest accomplishment.

•

Nintendo and Square's breakup in 1996 was fairly acrimonious. It is important to note that once it got out of the PC game business in 1987, Square had only developed games for Nintendo's platforms. Most third parties had at least dipped their toes into the Mega Drive (Sega Genesis) and PC Engine (TurboGrafx-16) markets in Japan and elsewhere, but never Square. Moreover, when it shifted to PlayStation development, it did so entirely, stopping production on everything for Nintendo platforms. But when Nintendo released its Game Boy Advance system in 2001, Square wanted back in. Although Nintendo at first refused Square's advances, in 2002 it announced that the companies had made up, and Square would begin developing Final Fantasy titles for Nintendo, although the main series remained on PlayStation hardware.

In 2005, after the release of the Nintendo DS, a portable that replaced the Game Boy line in the market, Square announced that it still had some tricks up its sleeve for the aging Advance: It would bring *Final Fantasy IV*, *V*, and *VI* to the system, nearly-perfect versions of the games with some extra features that could be played on the go. Nintendo announced in short order that the company itself would publish the games outside of Japan. And with that, *Final Fantasy V* was finally available in the West with a new translation befitting its greatness. It wasn't just that the new prose was well-edited, consistent with the series, and free of errors—it positively *sparkled* with humor and verve.

Since then, *Final Fantasy V* has been released a few other times. The PlayStation 1 version can be downloaded, warts and all, on the PlayStation 3, PlayStation Portable, and PlayStation Vita. There's a version for mobile phones, with redrawn high-resolution graphics and a touch interface. This version was also ported to the PC. Sadly, none of these releases are perfect. They've all got at least some flaws that the original Super Famicom game does not. It's arguable, depending on your priorities, that the best way to play *Final Fantasy V* in English is still to play the fan-translated ROM.

You don't even need to play it in an emulator, anymore. Hardware hackers have built readily available devices that store games on flash memory and plug directly into a Super Nintendo's cartridge slot. You can write the fan-translated game to an SD card and play it on original hardware. Some enterprising bootleggers have even gone so far as to create ersatz *Final Fantasy V* Super Nintendo cartridges, creating labels that look like Nintendo's authentic products and sometimes even cardboard boxes and manuals patterned exactly after the originals. You can buy one of these, pop open the shrink-wrap, and relive a past that never happened.

•

My first year in Japan, I was on a timer. After twelve months in Kanazawa, I had to return home and finish out my senior year at Tufts. But I'd had a taste of the good life, and I was ready to go back as soon as possible. I was fortunate enough to be selected for a Fulbright fellowship, and spent another year there after graduation, this time in Kyoto. The money ran out after a year, but if I wanted to make my own way there, I could. Some of my friends did. But in the end, I learned that there wasn't just one place in the world that I fit into perfectly. Japan made me appreciate America, too.

I went to Japan and came back. Some go to Japan and stay. Eric Koziol, a New Jerseyan who now lives in Nara prefecture in western Japan, moved there in 2006 the way many broke smart people do, on the Japan Exchange and Teaching (JET) Program, which places about 2,000 "young professionals" (usually recent college grads) per year in Japanese public schools as assistant language teachers.

The summer before his departure, Koziol wanted to get in some Japanese practice. So he turned to Final Fantasy. As an active member of NeoGAF, a popular video game internet forum, he noticed that a NeoGAF member who went by the handle "Red Scarlet" was doing a "Summer of Final Fantasy," playing through each game in turn and soliciting advice from other members about alternative ways to play through each one—"something new in an old favorite."

Koziol, who went by the handle "RevenantKioku," suggested that they both play *Final Fantasy V* simultaneously, and that they "backdraft" jobs to each other, like schoolyard picks. Each of them would assign ten of the game's twenty main jobs to each other, and they could only play through the game using those ten jobs. Whoever didn't get White Mage was going to have to get pretty clever about figuring out ways to restore hit points, in other words. In the end, the jobs they gave each other were fairly balanced, and both completed the game easily even though they only had access to half its features.

In 2008, with Koziol still living in Japan, he decided they should try a more difficult twist on the game. Five players would get four jobs each, and have to use only those jobs to finish the game. In 2009, he opened it up to any NeoGAF member who wanted to try. If they signed up, he'd assign them four random jobs, one for each of the game's crystals. "I just had a text file with all the jobs, and I sorted them out and randomized them," he says. He called it the "*Final Fantasy V* Four Job Fiesta."

What the Fiesta challengers soon discovered was that *Final Fantasy V* was a much deeper game than they'd originally thought. In restricting themselves to just four jobs, they were forced to study the ins and outs of the game's systems more closely than they had when they were powering through it using all the best strategies. Maybe they had to travel the world collecting Blue Magic. Maybe they discovered for the first time that Rods, the standard weapon for mages, could be "broken" in battle to unleash a single powerful spell regardless of the carrier.

Or, conversely, they might find that the classic Final Fantasy powerhouse fighters are the least advantageous when you have to carry them throughout the entire game. "The Knight is really boring," Koziol says. "You're basically just pressing Fight." The Dragoon, a character that can jump in the air away from the battle and come back down later with a powerful spear attack, is another dud in the Fiesta. "It's got good defense, but here's the thing," Koziol says. "You get a White Mage, Red Mage, Bard, and Dragoon. Okay, cool. The Dragoon jumps, and your highest defense character is in the air now. And all your weaklings are sitting on the ground taking punches." The Monk does a lot of bare-fisted martial arts damage in the early game, but gets relatively less effective as the game goes on.

What the four-job playthrough ends up teaching players is that it's the seemingly less powerful characters, the ones whose powers are more subtle, that turn out to be the best in a pinch. When Koziol and Red Scarlet first played their "backdraft" game, the other NeoGAF members laughed long and hard at Koziol receiving the Bard job class, which was considered to be useless. Much of this anti-Bard prejudice likely stems from the character Edward from *Final Fantasy IV*, a Bard who totally sucked. He dealt almost no damage and didn't do much else to support the party, a total gomer who had to be dragged from battle to battle. Edward was one of those *Final Fantasy* characters that make players cry when they *don't* die.

But the Bard in *FF5*? Stone-cold killer. If you learn the song "Requiem," you can do massive damage to undead enemies, which lets you easily level up in the zombie-filled Great Deep. There's also a powerful Bard song called "Hero's Song" that is cleverly hidden throughout the game. Each of the game's towns has a piano in its pub that you can play. As you find more pianos, the tunes Butz plays get better and better, from a clunky octave scale to a passable "Beautiful Dreamer" to Mozart to Debussy. After he finds the last piano, you learn "Hero's Song," which can be used in battle to raise your characters' levels temporarily.

Another surprisingly lucky draw in a Fiesta is the Chemist, whose main ability is mixing two consumable items together to create a new, more powerful item, which is immediately used in battle. "Chemist is basically considered a You Win," Koziol says. "It makes the game so much easier. You can raise your level and give yourself status effects that you can't get in other ways."

By 2011, the Four Job Fiesta was too popular for Koziol to continue to assign jobs by hand. So he built an automated script on his website that would spit out four different jobs for each player. But he was worried that unscrupulous players (or just plain trolls) would try to hack his website. "That's why I made it a charity event," he says. "If they screw around with a charity event, that's more of a dick move." Like a traditional charity walk, players of the Fiesta were asked to donate to the charity Child's Play, which benefits children's hospitals, or get their friends to donate for them. Some pledged flat amounts, some contingent on their successes and failures throughout the game. The first year, Four Job Fiesta raised $1,000. In 2016, thousands of players pulled in over $19,000 for the charity.

Today the Fiesta is a much more high-tech affair. Jobs are assigned to players via an automated Twitter account called "Gilgabot," and players often livestream their playthroughs on services like Twitch, which helps raise attention and bring in even more donations. Players can choose to play through any of the versions of the game they want, although the most popular seems to be the fan-translated Super Famicom version.

•

When the game was released, Sakaguchi and the Final Fantasy team believed that they themselves had already anticipated the many different strategies players might use to beat the game. This is rarely true of any video game, though, and is certainly not true of *Final Fantasy V*. Overseeing thousands of different playthroughs of the game each year, Eric Koziol has seen some truly amazing stuff. One technique used by speedrunners who attempt to get through *Final Fantasy V* in the fastest time possible is called "Death By Math." Level 5 Death isn't the only number-based Blue Magic spell in the game. There's "Level 3 Flare," for instance, which casts the game's strongest Fire spell on any enemy whose level is divisible by 3. There's also "Level 2 Old," which gives the "Old" status effect to any character whose level is an even number. "Old" can be used in conjunction with another Blue Magic spell called "Dark Shock," which halves an enemy's level, causing characters with odd levels to end up with even levels, so that you can give the "Old" status to any enemy, no matter how powerful. So what? Well, "Old" slowly ticks down a character's level over time. Through laborious trial and error, you can now pinpoint the exact moment that a character's level will tick down to a multiple of 5, cast Level 5 Death, and kill them. With math.

Probably the most difficult *Final Fantasy V* job to deal with in the Fiesta is the Berserker—a savage fighter.

Clothed in animal skins, all a Berserker can do is attack, and they are uncontrollable by the player. But they do huge damage, and they can wield large weapons like axes that do even more. Like the Monk, the Berserker's raw damage is helpful early in the game, but as things progress and enemies require strategies that are subtler and more nuanced, the Berserker becomes a liability.

But some clever players found workarounds even for that. There exists a piece of headwear called a Crown of Thorns that vastly increases a user's defense, but lowers their magic ability and causes their HP to constantly drain. But when equipped on a Berserker (usually with another accessory that counteracts the HP drain), something fascinating happens. Since the Berserker's Magic stat is so low already, the -5 to magic sends the stat into negative number territory. The Super Famicom can't deal with negative numbers, so what happens is just like what happened back in Hironobu Sakaguchi's college days, when he rolled his gold pieces in *Ultima II* from 9999 to 0. In this case, the Berserker's magic stat rolls back from 0 to 255.

Now you've got the most powerful magic caster in the entire game—but they can't cast magic. Enter the Gaia Hammer, a weapon that has a good chance of casting the spell Quake to all targets. Equip that on the Berserker, and it's pretty much a bloodbath. Starting in 2015, some players have actually been able to finish the final fight against ExDeath with four Berserkers using this strategy. Conquering the game using only these untamable beasts was the Fiesta's final frontier. It's truly possible, Koziol now believes, to finish the game using absolutely any combination of characters exclusively.

Andrew Vestal says that participating in the Four Job Fiesta is what gave him a renewed and deepened respect for *Final Fantasy V*. "I appreciated it a lot then, and I appreciate it a lot now, but the reasons I appreciate it are very different," he says. "I've come to understand the depth of the systems in a way that you don't really perceive in a single playthrough. As it loses its mythical status, I've been able to appreciate the game for its own merit, rather than seeing it as some kind of white whale."

•

Famitsu, the most popular Japanese gaming magazine, celebrated its 30th anniversary in the summer of 2016. To commemorate the occasion and look back on three decades of Japanese gaming history, the magazine asked its readers to answer a simple survey, *Family Feud* style: For each game platform of the last 30 years, select just one game that lingers in your memories.

The number one answer for Super Famicom, with 445 votes, was Nintendo's *Super Mario World*. The number two game was *Dragon Quest V*. And the number three answer was *Final Fantasy V*. More than *FF4*, more than *FF6*, it was the game that players instantly thought of when they thought back on the days playing the Super Famicom. "It was fun to search for the pianos in the towns," recalled one respondent, a 40-year-old woman. "And even though he's an enemy, I really like Gilgamesh."

It was a landmark game. It is prominent in the memories of those who lived through it. It introduced, or canonized, many of the elements that we now see as essential to the series: Moogles, Tonberi, countdown timers, superbosses. But because it missed out on being released anywhere but Japan when it was fresh and exciting in 1992, *Final Fantasy V* doesn't enjoy that reputation anywhere else. In the spring of 2017, the American gaming publications IGN and *Game Informer* both independently published lists titled "Top 100 RPGs of All Time." Coincidentally, the rankings of *Final Fantasy VI* and *Final Fantasy IV* on each list were almost identical: *FF6* ranked at #2 on each list, and *FF4* came in at #22 and #23, respectively. *Final Fantasy V* was not on either list.

•

Final Fantasy V was in many ways the last game of the first era of Final Fantasy. Most players familiar with the series would draw the line between *Final Fantasy VI* and *Final Fantasy VII*, and not without reason: That's when the developers shifted from sprites to polygons, from Super Famicom to PlayStation, from Yoshitaka Amano to Tetsuya Nomura.

But I'd draw the generational line between *FF5* and *FF6*. Whereas *Final Fantasy V* feels like an exceptional refinement of the designs and ideas of the first *Final Fantasy*, *FF6* feels like an attempt to separate itself from the old patterns. It's the first game to shed the strictly medieval castles-and-dragons setting for a less formulaic, almost steampunk world. It features lengthy, complex expository narrative sequences. It walks away from "crystals" as major elements of its world. And technologically and graphically, you can see the *FF6* team attempting to break through the limitations of the Super Famicom. Each scene tries in its way to get around the "grid of squares" graphic design that defined *Final Fantasy V* and all previous games, and attempts to create a more layered, rough-hewn, 3D, asymmetric world.

It's easy to imagine Hironobu Sakaguchi, upon the completion of *Final Fantasy V*, believing that he had perfected what he had set out to do with the first *Final Fantasy*, and moving on to a new challenge. What he left behind was in many ways the ultimate first-generation Final Fantasy. Andrew Vestal likens the experience to triple-distilled vodka: "They took everything that fans like about Final Fantasy and ran it through a filter, and what came out the other end was *Final Fantasy V*."

There simply isn't any other Final Fantasy like *Final Fantasy V*. While the job-change system was largely left behind in the main Final Fantasy series as the series became more character-driven and thus stricter with each character's occupations and ability sets, it does turn up in spin-off games like *Final Fantasy Tactics* and *Final Fantasy X-2*. But in these cases, it's nowhere near as intricate, nowhere near as customizable, as in *Final Fantasy V*. The utter complexity of the design makes it, from a gameplay perspective, as close to a *sui generis* experience as video games offer.

It is often noted that *Final Fantasy V* is the final Final Fantasy in which Hironobu Sakaguchi is credited as the game's director. He is credited as producer beginning with *Final Fantasy VI,* with his former title going to Yoshinori Kitase. Sakaguchi, for his part, waves away any notion that this signified a meaningful shift in his duties. "I thought that the ring of someone being called a 'producer' was really cool," he says. "So I said, you know what, I'm going to take over the title of 'producer,' and why don't you, Kitase, take the title of director? It probably didn't have any more serious consideration behind it. It was that kind of time."

•

In the West, *Final Fantasy V* feels like a game that fans adopted, took ownership of. An official version has been available for nearly eighteen years as of 2017, but the game is still so closely associated with emulators, with text files, with ripping out tabs, with Cara instead of Krile. While far more games, manga, and anime are translated and brought outside Japan today, that DIY spirit still strives to fill in the gaps with the ones that aren't, manifesting itself in ever more sophisticated ways. If a publisher makes a change to the localization that you don't like, you have more options than ever. Fans make their own remixes, adding "censored" content back in, or retranslating entire scripts. And if you don't want to do that, it's easier than ever to study Japanese with a bevy of free online tools.

"Otaku" is an ability, but it's not a job: It's a tool you carry with you, not a defining characteristic that excludes all other possibilities. You can get those mixed up and let a deep passion for a cultural interest lock you away from the world, or you can take that part of yourself and make it one aspect of a well-rounded person. It would be nice if we could simply rely on "official" channels to translate all the great manga, anime, and games into English, but that's simply impossible. We can all be ambassadors in some way, though, and help others share those experiences.

When I reconnected with Nora Stevens recently, she likened the experience of being an American otaku in the 1990s to being "on the other side of this very thin veil, and you're seeing this world of Japanese games and culture that are right there, and you can't get them."

"But, you know, we got really close," she says. "We were picking at it, bringing it over to our side, and we made it available for a lot of people. I'd like to think we really helped them." Nora's passion for Final Fantasy and Japan led her right into a localization career, working on the official English scripts for games like *Silent Hill 3* and *Kingdom Hearts II*. Andrew Vestal went into game localization as well, translating games like *Xenosaga* into English, and then joined Blizzard to oversee the localization (into many languages) of games like *Diablo III*. John Ricciardi, another American who imported *Final Fantasy V* back in the day and also wrote a FAQ, moved to Tokyo and founded the game localization company 8-4.

As for me, playing RPGs in Japanese was how I wedged a foot in the door of writing about video games, covering lots of imports with the added bonus of actually being able to understand what I was playing. The first piece I ever sold was on the subject of *Final Fantasy V*.

"It's like the joke that Brian Eno made about the album *The Velvet Underground & Nico*—it only sold

30,000 copies, but everyone who bought one started a band," Vestal says. "Only 5,000 people imported *Final Fantasy V* into the US, but all of them went on to work in the video game industry. For a certain person of a certain age, it was the sign of your dedication to video games as a medium."

JAPAN IS A PLACE YOU CAN GO. Your connecting flight is late, and two Japan Airlines attendees hustle you onto the wide-body 747 minutes before it takes off. You make it onto the plane. Your luggage does not. You're lucky you actually find a shirt that fits you in the shopping mall down the hill from your campus. With emergency clothing acquired, you can wander upstairs to where they keep all the video games, and buy a copy of *Final Fantasy IX*—a game not yet available in the place you came from.

You learn quickly and thoroughly that Japan is not just about video games and anime. Some of these lessons are surprising and joyful, and others come harder. You felt sure you belonged here, but now you're not sure at all. You definitely know that before the year is up, you want to buy all of the games that Square released on the Super Famicom. You are able to do this, at least, without feelings of ambiguity.

Soon enough the year is over, and it's time to drag your suitcases back down to the bus station and head to the airport. Thanks to an odd series of circumstances, you miss the airport bus, and will probably miss your flight. A kind woman who speaks impeccable English strikes up a conversation with you at the bus stop, and offers to let you share a taxi to the airport with her and her son, who sits next to you in the back seat of the cab. He's fourteen years old, visibly thrilled to be sitting next to you, and immediately begins peppering you with questions about the World Wrestling Federation, and which pro wrestlers you like.

"アメリカ、行きてー," he says finally, and you understand perfectly. "I want to go to America."

NOTES

A note on titles: Many games often underwent title changes when they were brought from Japan to the US *Final Fantasy IV* and *Final Fantasy VI* were originally retitled *Final Fantasy II* and *Final Fantasy III* here. Adding to the confusion, some games got a third title when they went to Europe. The Game Boy game *Seiken Densetsu: Final Fantasy Gaiden* was released in the US as *Final Fantasy Adventure* but called simply *Mystic Quest* in Europe. When *Final Fantasy Mystic Quest* was released in Europe, it was retitled *Mystic Quest Legend*.

All quotes from Hironobu Sakaguchi, Andrew Vestal, Nora Stevens, and Eric Koziol are from personal interviews conducted for this book in 2016. Hironobu Sakaguchi's quotes were expertly interpreted by Kyoko Higo, and I occasionally went back to re-translate his statements when a more exact wording was necessary.

Unless otherwise noted, quotes from *Final Fantasy V* are my own translations of the Super Famicom version's

Japanese text. English names of characters, places, and jobs are generally as they appear in the game's official Japanese strategy guides. The castle of Karnak, named for the Egyptian temples, was transliterated as "Karnac" in the Super Famicom guide, but changed to "Karnak" in the official Game Boy Advance version guide in 2006. Since this seems to have been a mistake that was corrected, we've used "Karnak" here.

The anecdote about Hironobu Sakaguchi and Hiromichi Tanaka's college years playing Western role-playing games is from an interview with Sakaguchi in the first volume of *Game Maestro*, a five-volume series of books published in 2000 and 2001 by Mainichi Communications in Japan.

The quote from Hisashi Suzuki and details about the early days of Square and Enix are from "The Birth of 'Final Fantasy': Square Corporation," published in English in the *Okayama Economic Review* volume 37, number 1, June 10, 2005.

My 2004 book, *Power-Up: How Japanese Video Games Gave the World an Extra Life*, which is referenced and quoted in the text, is currently available in a new 2016 edition from Dover Publications.

"Anime Culture Is Super-Cool!: The American Otaku Who Love Japan" (*Anime Bunka wa Chou Kakkoii!*) can be found in the Japanese magazine *Aera*, volume 8, number 44, October 2, 1995. Translations of direct quotes are mine. (This book's epigraph is also from this article, translation also mine.) I originally found the story of Toshio Okada and the Star Wars figures in a post by anime critic Carl Gustav Horn available here: http://bit.ly/2uM0twY (In researching this book, I confirmed with Horn that the post was his and the story was accurate.)

Some facts about the image of *otaku* around the world were drawn from Patrick W. Galbraith's essay "Akihabara: Conditioning a Public 'Otaku' Image" in Volume 5 of the journal *Mechademia* (2010, University of Minnesota Press).

The interview with Kazuko Shibuya originally appeared in Japanese at the website 4gamer, here (http://bit.ly/2ulmu4W), and is available in translation at Shmuplations (http://bit.ly/2vvWFh2).

The anecdote about *Actraiser*'s soundtrack and *Final Fantasy IV* comes from an interview with Nobuo Uematsu in the third volume of *Game Maestro*.

The 1997 interview in which Nobuo Uematsu discusses Irish music is in the liner notes of the audio CD *Final Fantasy VII Reunion Tracks*, released by Square Enix in Japan.

The 1993 interview in which Uematsu discusses ABP grinding in *Final Fantasy V* is appears in the Japanese magazine *The Super Famicom*, volume 4 number 3 (February 19, 1993) and volume 4 number 4 (March 5, 1993).

Jason Schreier, with whom I worked at WIRED and now at Kotaku, wrote an in-depth report on the making of the *Final Fantasy V* fan translation (http://bit.ly/2q9gMll), which I have used as a reference here. I also followed up with fan translation team member "Myria" (who went by the handle "Barubary" at the time of the *FF5* fan translation project) for a brief personal interview, quotes from which appear here.

An excellent, exhaustive comparison of the *Final Fantasy* and *Dungeons & Dragons* bestiaries can be found at http://bit.ly/2gTaanU.

The Tetsuya Nomura discussion of Tonberi and monster designs is from the fourth volume of *Game Maestro*. The quote about Nomura's notebooks is from a 2014 *Famitsu* magazine interview translated by the website Siliconera, and can be found at http://bit.ly/1m1MuZ6.

Mia Consalvo, the Canada Research Chair in Game Studies and Design at Montreal's Concordia University, devotes an entire chapter to fan translation in her excellent book *Atari to Zelda: Japan's Video Games in Global Contexts* (MIT Press, 2016), which was generally helpful.

The quote from Jeremy Blaustein is from a series of interviews by Bob Mackey for US Gamer titled "Tales from Localization Hell." http://bit.ly/2tpG8de

You can read the NeoGAF forum post in which the "Four Job Fiesta" concept originated at http://bit.ly/2uTB0Cs.

The Brian Eno quote that Andrew Vestal paraphrases originally appeared in *Musician* magazine's October 1982 issue. Here's the exact quote, which Eno concludes with a thought that I think is quite germane to our story, and that perhaps Hironobu Sakaguchi might appreciate:

> "My reputation is far bigger than my sales. I was talking to Lou Reed the other day and he said that the first Velvet Underground record sold 30,000 copies in the first five years. The sales have picked up in the past few years, but I mean, that record was such an important record for so many people. I think everyone who bought one of those 30,000 copies started a band! So I console myself thinking that some things generate their rewards in a second-hand way."

ACKNOWLEDGMENTS

I'm often given credit for "writing the first *Final Fantasy V* FAQ," but as you now know, it was a collaborative effort that I could never have accomplished on my own. So too was this book.

Many, many thanks to Hironobu Sakaguchi for carving out some time to speak with me about *Final Fantasy V*. This book changed so much in those 90 minutes, and I hope the fruits of our conversation were enlightening to all Final Fantasy fans. The same amount of thanks to Kyoko Higo, who arranged and interpreted the talk with Sakaguchi; her support was absolutely crucial to making the interview happen.

Jon Irwin, the author of the Boss Fight Books volume on *Super Mario Bros. 2*, indirectly planted the seeds of this project when he mentioned me in his book. I wasn't two pages into reading it when I realized I had to write one. Thanks to Gabe Durham for many things, but first for entertaining a wild pitch out of nowhere. Gabe and Michael P. Williams have been phenomenal editors, pulling apart each piece of the story and perfecting every line. As a full-time editor myself, I appreciate it. Imagine a surgeon having their appendix removed.

Thanks to those who consented to be interviewed for the project: Andrew Vestal, Eric Koziol, and Nora Stevens Heath. Thanks to my great friends Alexa Ray Corriea and Jeremy Parish for their feedback on early drafts. Thanks also to the many Boss Fight Books team members who came together to polish and perfect this book: cover designer Cory Schmitz, layout artist Christopher Moyer, copyeditor Ryan Plummer, and proofreaders Joseph Michael Owens and Nick Sweeney.

Finally, to my long-suffering family: Thanks to my parents for letting me give out their credit card number over the phone. And to my wife Regina—who, as a teen, started an AOL chatroom-based game titled "Final Fantasy Extreme" named after the cancelled SNES release of *FF5*—for her support of this extracurricular activity. And to my son Chris: Once you're old enough to read this, *do not stick pliers* into any of Dad's game consoles *unless* you're very sure something good will happen.

ALSO FROM
BOSS FIGHT BOOKS